The Daily Quest

Conquering a Sound Body, a Sane Mind, & a Soft Heart

Fox Lehjika

ISBN: 9781791765385

Prologue

Life on earth is a dichotomic gamble. Either we live, or we die. If we die, the equation is solved. But if we are alive, there are two possibilities: either we are happy, or we are unhappy. If we are happy, there are little things to worry about and few questions to ask. If we are unhappy, there two possibilities: either we get to work to reverse our misfortune, or we bow to the challenge. If we give up trying, we can just sit and wait for the nature to take care of us and relegate life concerns until eventually death comes. If we are resilient and keep fighting for a better life, there are two possibilities: either we choose to be constructive, or we engage in destructive schemes. In either situation, we find ourselves faced with many questions and few or no answers. Some questions raising hope, some others striking fear and uncertainty. If we find answers, some solve our problem with no collateral damage to ourselves and to others; some others go the other way. In both cases, these answers can be like medication; curing some patients and hurting others, and sometime bringing both cure and harm at the same time!

In some instances, we intend to do good, just to end up with harmful results. In some other cases, ill intentions result in something good. In all these situations, one thing remains a constant; that is, nothing is certain and there is no guarantee that the next hour will find us in physical, mental, and emotional shape to face the next challenges or seize on new opportunities.

The search for such certainty is elusive, which makes it a **Daily Quest**. The underlying question, which is the cornerstone of this book, becomes: what can we do to ensure that our journey in this dichotomous web of life can be pursued without losing the equilibrium of our body, mind, and heart, these being the most important instruments we need for the Quest, but also the most vulnerable to life constrains? Let us explore the tools nature has provided to help us answer this question. May we all find them valuable, learn how to harness their tremendous power, and successfully use them in our **Daily Quest**.

Contents

INTRODUCTION

We wake up every morning with one main goal: having a good day; a good day meaning being happy, achieving success, having good times with family and friends. But, on the flip side of this goal, looms a shadow of doubt, uncertainty, and fear of the unknown; that is, the unforeseeable events that might occur in the next hour, day, week, etc....Above the whole sense of achieving our goals and in the depth of our hearts, we are highly concerned with our physical, mental, and emotional health, for the very goal we wake up with depends on how sound our physical body is, how sane our mind is, and how soft our heart is. From the core of our being, we daily and constantly yearn for assurance and answers to the questions: how certain are we to be healthy in the next hour? How much does the achievement of our life's goals depend on us being healthy and how does health influence our happiness and success in life? What price are we willing to pay to conquer a healthy body, mind, and heart? Pretending to offer a satisfactory answer to these questions may sound overly ambitious.

Yet, the answers exist. On the one hand, were there a onetime answer to these concerns, a onetime price could be paid, and the problem could be settled once and for all. But, just as these life pressing questions come to us and need to be answered on daily basis, the likely answers require a sustained daily application, on the other hand. Finding and applying these solutions is our Daily Quest.

Every one of us is born, grows up, and lives in an environment which constantly brings opportunities and challenges, but also provides a context within which we experience the ups and downs; from repeated failures, breakdowns, trials and retrials, to joyfully achieving success in our enterprises. Further, we all have people, beliefs, and systems that we depend on when dealing with life questions, which we also influence in return. Finally, and more importantly, we all have a physical body, a mind, and emotions the quality of which can never be taken for granted, but which largely influence our pursuit for happiness and our ability to achieve life goals. We find ourselves compelled to a daily evaluation of the context in which we function, including all factors that impact, enhance, or limit our ability to achieve our personal, social, spiritual, or other goals.

From the time we are born, we begin our life experience by learning skills that shape our ability to successfully interact with the visible world around us and the invisible forces within and around us. The first thing we are taught is to learn how to FOCUS; to CONCENTRATE our attention to ourselves and the surroundings. As newborn, we come in a new world where everything is so new to us that we tend to grab whatever our little hands can reach. As time goes by, we slowly, but consistently learn how to deploy our five senses to interact with the outside environment. Eventually, everything becomes progressively so natural, so normal that our newly developed skill of concentration becomes a necessary companion, at the same time as we begin to grasp its value, but also the trouble to master it.

As we grow up, the importance for us to focus our mind follows us through our first days at school and, as we reach our adult life, it is embedded in and intrinsically connected to everything we do; whether it is taking a shower, playing a game, cooking meals, organizing a room, driving an automobile, or designing and managing a complex project. Thus, we realize how important staying focused contributes to our wellbeing and to success in our enterprises. In the end, we become self-conscious of the value of concentration and we don't need to be reminded how much achieving goals and happiness in life depend on our capacity to stay focused. Moreover, as experiences shape our approach to life, we understand the connection between our capacity to focus and the sanity of our mind; that is, the clearer our mind, the less confused or frustrated we are. In short, we are naturally predisposed to focus our mind and the necessity of life stresses that we consistently, increasingly, and persistently practice **Concentration**.

Secondly, at the same time we were learning how to concentrate, another stress was placed on our ability to organize, ponder, think critically, analyze, and present our thoughts to ourselves and to others in orderly and logical ways. We also learned how to apply our thoughts to coordinate our actions and to understand, frame, and solve problems. During childhood, we learned how to solve puzzles and build our first Lego house or car. Later, we engaged in activities and exercises that involved abstract theorems at high school and college, and we learned how to manage high volumes of increasingly complex workloads, while we were developing the skills of judgement and ponderance. We also learned how to think things over and to apply a variety of solutions to solve simple and complex issues. Our capacity to discern and to explain HOW and WHY things work or don't work grew at the equivalent pace. When we have a clear understanding of problems and we know how to find appropriate solutions to them, our mind clarity becomes a *Remedy* against the shadows of confusion, which is a fertile ground for frustration, stress, and breakdown. In many respects, this process, like Concentration, is as inherent to our human nature as it is necessary and has nothing of extraordinary or transcendental nature. Without prejudice to the details to come, let's call this process **Meditation**, or Med-itation.

Finally, as we were learning how to stay focused (Concentration), to ponder (Meditation) on our thoughts and actions, we also learned how to deploy our personality and individuality to interact with and influence the outside world. This interaction brings us face to face with life challenges and opportunities. Some days we achieve success, some others we bend to failure. When either of these realities of life occur, we reach out to others to either celebrate and share the joys for our achievements, to ask for help and support, or to seek comfort for our pains, failure, and losses. We also enjoy the company of others to either compete for success or for fun, to express gratitude for good deeds received, to praise, and congratulate others for their achievements, or to forgive them for their wrongdoings. In many other situations, the company of people, communities, and societies allows us to receive gratitude, praise, and congratulations for our good deeds, qualities, and achievements, and provides us with a venue to repay our debts, to redeem ourselves, but also to ask for and receive forgiveness for our mistakes and wrongdoings that adversely affect others. In some other times, however, whether we experience joy or sorrow, we rather introvert our thoughts and feelings to find a source of comfort and support from within ourselves. In other instances, we direct our thoughts and feelings to both inside and outside sources to talk to ourselves, or to pray for comfort and support. This whole thing is what is called relationship. There is no need to discuss the value of a good relationship and its benefit on our physical, mental, and emotional health. It is for this reason that a good relationship is a healthy relationship and a bad one is an unhealthy relationship. Let's call this process of interaction with other people and with ourselves **<u>Prayer.</u>**

As will be discussed and expanded in chapter three, when we engage in the above listed three processes we naturally, but also intrinsically practice Concentration, Meditation, and Prayer. These exercises are the most important, but often ignored or underused, tools we possess to keep our system moving. We all, in one way or another, consciously or unconsciously concentrate, meditate, and pray as a part of our human nature and by necessity of life. From this perspective, it can be said that everybody concentrates, meditates, and prays. We use and acknowledge these practices as NATURAL processes of life. There is basically no need for religion and gurus for us to focus our mind, to think critically, and to engage in healthy interactions with others. What is needed, however, and what this discussion is about, is learning how to harness the power of these three exercises to maximize the benefit of their power in our physical, mental, and emotional health. Success and happiness in life depend upon the soundness of our body, the sanity of our mind, and the softness of our heart. Building and keeping such a healthy system is as important to us as it is a fragile thing that needs to be conquered on daily basis; that is, it is a Daily Quest.

To learn how to harness the power of Concentration, Meditation, and Prayer, this essay will cover the following points in three chapters:

Chapter 1] Unfolding the Inner Power,

Chapter 2] The Creative Power of Thought,

Chapter 3] Gearing up for the Quest.

This way, by the end of this exchange, we will become able to understand what the Inner Power is and how it relates to each individual; the importance of Thought Power; and the value of harnessing the power of Concentration, Meditation, and Prayer as the Gears we need in our Daily Quest to conquer a Sound Body, a Sane Mind, and a Soft Heart. Instead of being reactive to the flow of life's events, we can set ourselves out for a conscious effort to train our will power to control our destiny.

Chapter 1
Unfolding the Inner Power

The first step in harnessing the power of Concentration, Meditation, and Prayer is to consider the existence of the *Inner Power*. This is something of which most of us either have no knowledge, or neglect to consider, or which we simply do not even suspect the existence. Nevertheless, the Inner Power is a stupendous factor in human life and the one upon which everything, including our life on earth, is most dependent. Paul the Apostle makes high reference to the Inner Power when he stated in one of his correspondences with the Corinthians that: *"who knows a person's thoughts except their own spirit within them? In the same way no one knows the thoughts of God except the Spirit of God"*. ([1])

The Inner Power is our individual Force from Within, the Inner God; that is, the vitalizing force, which is part and identical to the very source from which everything in our universe proceeds; the essential power that sustains us and the universe and keeps us going. We naturally refer

---

[1] 1 Corinthians 2:11

1

to this Inner Power as *I, ME*, and we use the possessive adjective and pronoun MY and MINE to convey the difference between possessions and the possessor. This is the truth everyone expresses when we say: "my body, my heart, my mind, my thoughts, my desires", etc... Our thoughts, feelings, and body make our personality, but it is the Inner Power that gives each of us a distinguished individuality. We may share same thoughts, feelings, and physical resemblance with many people from different places and times; we may even share same DNA with thousands of other people, but everyone has something that can neither be copied, duplicated, nor shared to resemble that of another; the force that gives the personality its uniqueness. This special thing is THE INNER POWER or THE INNER GOD.

From the introverted perspective, the Inner Power is our individual God Within, and the God Within is part the God of the Universe, the cosmic force from which all things spring. It is our personal link to the Power of the Universe. Therefore, we can see how powerful this Inner Power is, for this is our God Within; our True Self. The Inner Power is *omnipotent,* because it is a part of the God of the Universe. It is also *omniscience,* because just as God of the Universe is the Great Intelligence that knows everything about the world, the Inner Power knows everything about our personality and individuality in which it enfolds. These attributes of omnipotence and omniscience, however, are more or less latent in humanity at the present time. It is the function of evolution to unfold them into positive, dynamic expressions. This is what we are gradually learning to do in our daily lives and experiences, but this unfolding can be accelerated by undertaking the Quest as explained later.

The Inner Power affects our personality and the daily life in many ways: first, it is constantly sending messages down into our conscious mind. We call this INGENUITY, which from Latin means *"born from within"*. These messages appear as intuitions, inspirations, and original ideas. They tell us what the Inner Power, in its wisdom, wishes us to do to solve problems and bring about life changes, or to answer the many questions we may have. If we follow these suggestions and put them into effect, the results in our lives will be constructive. Failure will be changed into success, the obstacles which have beset us will gradually disappear, and we shall find that everything begins to work together for good and for success in every department of life. If, on the other hand, we ignore the directives from the Inner Power and follow the self-indulgent desires and straying thoughts of the personality, then we shall find that our troubles will increase and our pathway through life will become more difficult.

Human history is full of factual proofs of how this transformative and constructive force, as it was followed through, has changed the world from the primitive stage to modernity. And we are not there yet; as humanity we still have a long path to go; with many opportunities for many failures, mistakes, and shortcomings before we can realize the full potential of our Inner Force. Therefore, it is very important that we remain on the alert to catch the ideas and intuitions of the Inner Power and then put them into effect. Everyone can most effectively receive these messages by quieting the conscious mind, and particularly by having quiet times for concentration, meditation, or prayer so that when the conscious mind is stilled, the Inner Power can speak to us and we can hear it. Just as a server or a transmitter constantly sends messages to a receiver, so does the Inner Power constantly speak to us and send us mental messages all the time, no matter how active, busy, or distracted we may be. But, just as the receiver will capture the message from the transmitter when the former is turned on, so can our conscious mind record the Inner Power's messages when it is more receptive.

The second way the Inner Power sends us messages is through our CONSCIENCE, or an inner feeling or voice viewed as acting as a guide to the rightness or wrongness of one's behavior, and which we should always do well to obey. If only we follow the directions of this Power, it will speak to us in ever-clearer tones, gradually reshaping our lives and transforming our failures into successes. We must cultivate belief in the existence of the Inner Power and belief in its ability to transform our lives. This belief, as explained in the last chapter, is the wire, the electrical circuit that connects our conscious mind to the Inner Power. If we establish a clear connection between these two poles of our being, the result will be very much better, because then the Inner God can send messages to the mind and the latter can receive them much more clearly and effectively. Disbelief in these things impairs the connection and, in some respects, even destroys it. In such cases, we are left more or less without the conscious guidance and wisdom of the Inner God, and we easily run amuck, trailing failure with us. Let's make it crystal clear that believing in the expansive powers of the Inner God is not a matter of mere affirmations or denials. Many of us make a lot of statements of faith in the Inner Power or faith in ourselves, while not following through. Many others would like to deny the existence of anything that can be associated with religious beliefs, but, in truth, they are more connected to their God Within than they admit. What matters is that we establish the connection with and we are receptive to the Inner Power. Thus, we will see that this belief is of great importance. Some people call it faith - faith in God, a subject we will discuss in detail later.

For now, let us only say that faith in the Inner God and its power is the same thing as faith in the omnipotence and omniscience God of the universe. If we listen to and obey the suggestions and directions of the Power Within, fear and anxiety are taken away and we gain poise, which largely contribute to good health and is a factor in material success. We lose our fear of both life challenges and death. We know that all things are ordered with wisdom and that they will turn out well from the cosmic point of view. Moreover, we can increase the good results by praying to, talking with, conversing with the God Within, because this force is right here, nearer than our very breathing.

As will be seen in Chapter 3, talking to the Inner Power is the same thing as what religion calls praying to God. This, contrary to common claim, is not a mere religious performance, because it is a natural exercise, we all practice as a matter of normality. After all, religion put aside, everybody talks to "themselves". Religions have, however, tried to religionize this, but have also extroverted this exercise by making prayer an address to a power from outside; an exterior God. Thus, religions turn followers' attention to a God from outside, while the natural way is to talk to the God from Within. But, whether introverted or extroverted, this is the same thing. It is nevertheless better that we get to know the Power from Within, just as Carl Jung said: *"Who looks outside, dreams; who looks inside, awakes."*

As elaborated later, when we talk to the Inner Power, either mentally or in words, we may tell it what our ideals and ambitions are, what we wish to accomplish, and what we would like to have. Then leave the materialization to the Inner Power and not make the mistake of demanding this or that thing. When we have finished the conversation, we have made the thought form and in due time it will be materialized for us in such form and to such degree as the Inner God deems wise, particularly if we repeat it from time to time. We should be happy with this, knowing that it embodies the highest wisdom. If we do the above, we are *living by faith*. By living serenely in the knowledge of the existence of this Inner Power and having belief or faith that it will work out a perfect result in our lives, all the guilt of the past will fade away, anxiety for the present will evaporate, and fear for the future gradually will disappear, as we gain in confidence, poise, and tranquility. Therefore, living by knowledge-based faith in the Inner Power is not only a healthy mental and emotional undertaking, but it also increases our material success and makes us much happier. Thus, by establishing a constant connection with our Inner Power, by becoming receptive to the messages it sends to our conscious mind, and by placing our faith in its omnipotence and omniscience, we allow our true self to reveal itself and to pour its dynamic power in our entire life through increased opportunities to fully enjoy the benefits of a sound body, a sane mind, and a soft heart. In sum, even when we walk in the dark, we can be assured that the Inner God always shows us the way by illuminating the path of the Creative Power of Thought.

Chapter 2
The Creative Power of Thought

The second most important factor to consider in this Quest, and one that is the determinant of human progress and place in the universe, is the Creative Power of Thought.

Now that we have become familiar with the concept of the Inner Power, we are prepared to understand that the destiny of humankind is to become creator, not just imitator. The power to create is latent in each of us. Through the work of evolution, we are being progressively transformed from static to dynamic creators, in the likeness of the Universal Creative force, or God from whom we all emanated. In this respect, our Thought is probably the most significant, yet least understood, factor in our lives. When we look within ourselves, we cannot go very far before we are forced to recognize the fact that a power having vast possibilities dwells within us; that is, the Thought-power.

Our ideas take shape as mental pictures that we form with increasingly great facility and, afterwards, crystallize into material things in an exceedingly slow and laborious manner as cities, houses, machines, institutions, etc. Consequently, no one can deny the truth that all that is made by human hands is crystallized thought.

When we consider the slow mode of manifestation from thought to things as an indication of the many possibilities the Thought has, we should also admit the fact that if it escapes and eludes us, it can cause dismay. These possibilities and capabilities have been demonstrated by other forces we have already harnessed to our wheels of progress. For example, for countless ages the waves of the ocean wasted energy in beating upon the seashore, but once the human mind confronted the mysteries and myths and removed the shadows of fear and death that surrendered the mechanic of waves, the power of human mind harnessed them by coupling the waterfall to the electric dynamo. For alike period, the winds swept the land and sea before the human mind learned how to use them as carriers of international commerce by appropriate sailing vessels and as generators of electricity for our homes and workplaces. Along the same line, and for many years, steam escaped into the air from the camp kettles of primitive humanity before the power of human thought learned how to concentrate the power of the steam and use it in various industries. Following the same suit and for ages, we marveled at the beauty of sunlight and enjoyed warm weather, but now we are transforming this source of power to generate renewable and clean electricity and slowly replacing the old ones.

As we can learn from traditions and religions of ancient civilizations, the forces of earth, wave, wind, and sun were considered to be the manifestation of either gods or devil spirits, and therefore worshipped or feared for their devastating capabilities. Paracelsus, one of the forefathers of modern medicine, classified them as *Elementals*: gnomes (earth), undines (water), salamanders (fire) and sylphs (air). But, once the human mind became receptive to the tune of the Inner Power, the creative human *ingenuity* (or knowledge born from within) found a way to extract from these natural forces something of great utility for our lives. It is, however, worth noting that though the we have come to know and have made the forces of the wave, wind, and sunlight useful to us, the forces that reside beneath our Earth are still largely

11

unknown to us and therefore more feared. Most of us walkabout the Earth and see only a seemingly dead mass, but once an earthquake strikes, even the most courageous among us would not escape the feeling of being shaken in our very soul. Moreover, though the spectacle of a volcanic eruption can marvel our heart and take us in some sort of ecstatic admiration of the fiery phenomenon, to many of us, the devastations and dramatic havoc it brings can easily cast in our soul the images of an infernal abyss.

To this day, modern scientists still know very little about the mysteries of the Earth. So far as seismic phenomena are concerned, they have, with all their usual splendid care, investigated the very outside shell, but only to an insignificant depth. As for volcanic eruptions, they still try to understand them as coming from the center of the Earth, which they say is a fiery furnace. But, like Doctor Faust seeking to unlock the mysteries of life was rejected by the spirit of the Earth, our scientists are still struggling to explain the tremendous forces of the Earth and, needlingly, their usefulness to the benefit of human civilization. Until now, we have allowed the energies from inside Earth to escape and to threaten us. But, just with the other previously listed forces, the Power of human

Thought will remove the veil covering the mystery of the Earth forces and learn how to utilize them. Accordingly, just as all these energies escaped uselessly from the kettles of olden time, so does the radiant energy of Thought escape from us to this day; and just as we discovered the usefulness of the other forces and learned how to utilize them by capturing, concentrating, and controlling them, so can also this subtler, but enormously more potent Thought-Power be concentrated and put to work with a facility impossible of imagination even by comparison with the other forces, for they are merely utilitarian, working in, with and upon already existing things, but Thought-Power is a CREATIVE FORCE already in our possession.

On the other hand, we know how dangerous the forces from waves, wind, steam, and sunlight are when harnessed and concentrated. If the steam escapes from the camper's kettle it can do no serious hurt. Electricity generated by the friction of a belt or by rubbing a piece of amber is no danger to anyone. But when steam is generated in quantities and confined in a steam boiler, it may burst its bonds in the hands of an incompetent or careless worker, so may electricity under pressure in a wire kill the one who ignorantly meddles with it. Similarly, we may infer that

Thought-Power misdirected or ignorantly used would have a far more disastrous effect, because it is a much subtler force. Therefore, it is necessary that we should be placed in a school where we can learn to use this enormous force in a safe and efficient manner. This school is our concrete existence, the daily life. Whether we know it or not, every day, every hour we are here learning the lesson of RIGHT THOUGHT and as we learn it, more and more we shall become creators like God, the expansion of whom is our Inner Power.

The overreaching power of human thought is set out of unbelievable developments in coming years. The use and expression of this power does not depend upon outside machinery, which cost money and could be controlled by the wealthy and powerful; all humans, without exception possess this power from birth to death. For now, the nature and use of Thought-Power may sound or is yet a higher ideal than even a central power station. But the time is coming when there will be no need for elevators when everybody can levitate at will; no need of cars or railways when everybody can move swiftly and easily by his/her own inherent force; no need of ships and planes when we can move through the water and air without such cumbersome contrivances as compared to today's technologies. But, as mentioned before, like all other forces, Thought-Power could be used as a means of destruction and it will swift in that also. Therefore, exceeding care would naturally be required of one who uses it. S/he must have self-control in highest degree, for if s/he were to give way to temper dire disaster would surely happen. If ever we are to use such a force as that, we can see how essential it will be that we be good and kind and make no enemies, because our lives would be in the hands of others to an extent undreamt of now. Therefore, conquering a Soft Heart is paramount to our development, along with a Sound Body and a Sane Mind.

If we consider the processes of our Thought, it is generally believed to be a purely private and personal matter. Even at this stage of human development, we are still in a large measure unaware of the complicated ramifications and consequences of even the most seemingly insignificant thoughts formed in our minds. To illustrate the importance of thought, however, it's not an overstatement to contend that everything that exists in the universe was first a thought, for Thought is a Creative Power.

Many mythologies, tales, and legends from different cultures and religions of the world have stories about the creation of the universe. A common story is that there was a time when darkness reigned supreme; everything we now perceive and know was then non-existent, or at least not as organized as we have come to know it. Earth, oceans, and the heavenly bodies that illuminate the sky were not yet formed; neither were the multitudinous forms that live and move upon the various planets. All was yet in a fluidic condition and the Cosmic energy brooded quiescent in limitless space as the One Existence. The ancient Greeks called that condition of homogeneity CHAOS. Then came the state of orderly segregation, which we now see in the marching orbs that illumine the vaulted canopy of the sky, the stately procession of planets around central stars, the majestic Suns; the unbroken sequence of the seasons and the unvarying alternation of tidal ebb and flow; all this aggregate of systematic order was called COSMOS and was said to have proceeded from Chaos.

The ancient Greeks' cosmology has inspired and continue to influence our understanding of how the universe came in existence. The traces of such influence can be found in literatures of the early Christianity. In fact, one of the most informative, but also the most misinterpreted truth about the relationship between Chaos and Cosmos can be found in the first five verses of the gospel by St. John (²). Like any person who is reverently communicating with the Inner Power and seeks to acquire understanding of the mysteries of life, Saint John seems to have transcended the form-side of things and found himself in the presence of the God Within - standing in the realm of Abstract Thought and seeing the eternal verities we now take for granted, thanks to the power of science and human ingenuity.

Let's take a moment to examine the fundamental meaning of words used by St. John to clothe the prelude to his Gospel, which, and this is important to point out, was originally written in the Greek language - a much simpler matter than is commonly supposed, for Greek words have been freely introduced into our modern languages, particularly in scientific terms - and to show how this ancient teaching is supported by the latest discoveries of modern science.

The opening of St. John's Gospel reads: *"In the*

---

² Gospel by Saint John

BEGINNING was the WORD and the WORD was with GOD, and the WORD was GOD. The WORD was with God in the beginning. Through it all things were made; without it nothing was made that has been made". There is no need to quarrel on the interpretation the church has given to these verses with respect to the term WORD, which the popular Christian church considers as the same as Jesus, whom it says to have existed before all things and have created all things. However, an orthodox reading of the Greek terms for BEGINNING, WORD, and GOD, the context of these words in the Greek cosmology, as well as recent scientific discoveries shine a different light on the prelude of St. John's gospel.

Let's start with the term BEGINNING in the opening sentence of the Gospel by Saint John. BEGINNING was translated from the Greek word ARCHE, of which Aristotle refers to as *Elementary Condition*, *First Principle*, *Primordial Substance*, *Actuating Principle*, or a *Cause* ([3]). For one thing, science and religion agree in teaching that all things were formed from one homogeneous substance. It is that basic principle that John

---

[3]https://www.encyclopedia.com/humanities/encyclopedias-almanacs-transcripts-and-maps/arche

called ARCHE, primordial matter. The dictionary defines archeology as "the science of the origin (ARCHE) of things. Arche is also a root word for Archives, Archangel, and many other words, but the most consequential of them in this respect is the term ARCHITECT. The second term used by John is God. God is considered the Grand Builder of the universe. The Greek term for Builder is TEKTON, which also means, technician. When associated with the word ARCHE "primordial matter", we get the noun ARCHITECT, and this makes perfect sense that not only the ancient Greeks, but all ancient and modern religions call God the Chief Architect or ARCHITEKTON, or the Creator, the Builder, the Technician of the Primordial Matter. The third important term used by St. John is WORD, which was also translated from the Greek LOGOS. The term Logos has been used to mean not simply "word", but also to refer to any general word-construction; a theory or an account of something, or an idea or concept. While it's a bit of a stretch to use the term WORD for a theory or systematic account, such as we might find in biology or chemistry, or in philosophy, that broader use of the Greek Logos was a natural extension of their term. As we have learned, the word 'biology', for example, comes directly from the Greek BIOS meaning "life" plus Logos. Biology is therefore the theory of life. Moreover, from the term LOGOS we get the derivation of the term Logic. Etymologically speaking, Logic is anything pertaining to Logos. To call something "logical" is to say that it's something that we can understand. To be logical means to put something in sensible words, and where we have words, we have concepts; we have thought. It is in this connection to concepts, thought and human understanding that we find the importance of the term Logos. Thus, we see that when the opening sentence of St. John's Gospel is properly translated, it means that in the ARCHE (prime matter) there was LOGOS (a Concept, a Thought), which came from TEKTON (the Thinker, God). The combination of Arche, Logos, and Tekton is the chief source of all things, because for anything to come into existence, as it can be seen in human creative process, there must be a Thinker, (TEKTON, God) who generates Thought (Logos). Then the Thought (Logos) is sent into the Prime Matter (Arche) as a Creative Fiat to organize, model, and systematize it, and once put in an orderly mode, the Primordial Matter (Arche) with all things it contains enfolds the force of the Thinker, (Tekton, God).

This interpretation aligns well with the ancient Greeks cosmology. According to it, first there was CHAOS (from the ancient Greek Khaos meaning a state of no order, an abyss or a void) in the Primordial Matter (Arche). Then came Logos (concept, thought, system) to introduce order - LOGIC - into Chaos. Finally, the work of Logos on Chaos produced COSMOS or Universe (from the ancient Greek *kosmos* meaning an orderly arrangement or adornment). All this was planned and executed by Tekton, the builder.

The concept of LOGOS is one of the most important in that when we add the term ARCHE as used by St. John, we get a clear understanding of the BEGINNING of a LOGICALLY arranged Universe emerging from CHAOS. To say that Cosmos came out from Chaos is to validate the fact that in the Arche (primordial state of matter), Logos was needed as the bringer of an orderly arrangement of movements, vibrations, and rhythm in the Abyss. Logos organized, systematized, and enlightened the universe as far as we know it. And because there is a system of ideas organizing the universe, then in principle it is possible for us humans to discover and understand that system of ideas and thus

21

the universe itself. From this view, the Logos, or WORD, is truly the light that shines in the world, but the world does not get it, as St. John concludes in the 5th verse of his prelude. So, when properly translated, the teaching of John both fully embodies the above arguments and aligns with science, for the Greek term LOGOS means both the reasonable thought (we also say logic) and the Word or Sound - Wave - that expresses this logical thought. A slight study of the science of sound shows us that a sound is vibration and that different sounds will mold sand or other light materials into figures of varying form. A Sound has that capacity to create or bring order in an otherwise chaotic mass.

To bridge the religious and scientific reading of St. John's cosmogenesis verses, we may say:

1- In the ARCHE, (primordial substance that emerged from Chaos), there was LOGOS, (logical, orderly arrangement of elements, or creative cosmic waves).

2- The LOGOS (logical order) came from and was with the Thinker (TEKTON, God).

3- The LOGOS (logical order) was in the ARCHE (primordial substance) with the Thinker - TEKTON; God.

4- From this prime fact, our universe has come into

existence, and nothing exists apart from that fact, because LOGOS, as a Creative Fiat, reverberates through space and segregates the homogeneous prime substance into separate forms; from galaxies to microbes, all things that populate the universe.

This is not an attempt to somehow arbitrarily delegitimize the church's interpretation of the gospel (which holds as matter of faith for the church), but it is self-evident that the term LOGOS (word, logical order) does not stand alone and is not the same as the term Beginning, because a Thought must precede a Word and a Thinker must generate Thought before the latter can be expressed into Word. In the same line, the very fact that all cultures and religions talk about a state of emptiness that preceded the creation of the universe and that the creation of such universe is attributed to a Supreme Being, God, who did so by pronouncing the creative word, shows that LOGOS was not the beginning of all things, but proceeded from the Creator, and that the universe did not come from nothing, but from Chaos.

This interpretation is not far removed from recent scientific experiments by LIGO [4] on the detection and measurement of the Gravitational Waves. The LIGO experiment shows that an important trace of the Big Bang is the cosmic microwave background. Science considers this Cosmic Microwave as a "radiation left over from the birth of the universe, created about 300,000 years after the Big Bang. But the birth of our universe also created gravitational waves, and these would have originated just a fraction of a second after the event. The waves with the highest frequencies may have originated during phase transitions of the primitive universe or by vibrations and snapping of cosmic strings" ([5]). The catching of such waves will revolutionize cosmology, giving us crucial information about how the universe came to be, and will eventually provide us with an empirical proof of the implications of the terms Arche, Logos, and God as used by St. John, as well as how this trinity is enfolded in and ensouls the universe with all it contains.

The general idea is to consider Chaos and Cosmos as superlative antitheses of each other. But, as seen previously, according to the ancient Greeks and based on the Latin maxima *"Ex Nihilo, Nihil Fit"*, or nothing can come from

---

[4] https://www.ligo.org/science/GW-Stochastic.php

[5] https://phys.org/news/2017-07-giant-atoms-gravitational-big.html#jCp

nothing, Chaos was necessary before COSMOS was made possible in its ARCHE state by the resounding LOGOS. If we put religion, science, and the antic cosmology together, we can assume that the first thing the Supreme Being did was to "think out," or imagine, the Universe before the beginning of active manifestation, everything, including the millions of Solar Systems and the web of great creative schemes that unfold as an expansion of the Supreme Being's conscience. The second assumption of what the Supreme Being did is that which manifests in matter as the forces of attraction and cohesion, thus giving it the capability of combining into Forms of various kinds. This was done so by spelling out "The Word", the "Creative Fiat," which molds the primordial Cosmic Root-substance in a manner similar to the formation of figures by musical vibrations. In this respect, if for example, we place two tuning-forks of exactly same pitch next to each other, and if we strike one of them, the sound will induce the same vibration in the other, weak to begin with, but if the strokes are continued, the second fork will give out a louder and louder tone until it will emit a volume of sound equal to that of the first. This will happen though the forks are several feet apart, and even if one of them is encased in glass. The sound from the smitten one will penetrate the glass and the answering note be emitted by the enclosed instrument. These invisible sound-vibrations have great power over concrete matter. They can both build and destroy. In the same token, if a small quantity of very fine powder is placed upon a brass or glass plate, and a violin bow drawn across the edge, the vibrations will cause the powder to assume beautiful geometrical figures. The human voice is also capable of producing these figures; the same tone always producing the same figure. This is the true nature of the great primordial *LOGOS*; "the Only Begotten", which when it was first spelled out by the Supreme Being, brought in the finest matter all the different solar systems and galaxies, with all their myriads of forms, which have since been copied and worked out in detail by the innumerable creative forces.

But, "the Word" could not have done this, however, until the Supreme Being had first prepared the Cosmic Root-substance; had awakened it from its normal state of inertia and set the countless *interconnected* atoms spinning upon their axes, placing those axes at various angles with respect to each other, giving to each kind a certain measure of vibration. These varying angles of inclination of the axes and the measures of vibration made the Cosmic Root-substance capable of forming different combinations, which are the basis of the great universe we live in today.

Physics and astronomy teach us that there is in each part of the universe and its unnumbered solar systems a different inclination of the axes, and a different measure of vibration. Consequently, the conditions on each one and their combinations are different from those in any of the others, due to the activity of the "Only Begotten WORD." After all, there is only one force in the universe; God, the Great TEKTON of the ARCHE, the Great Architect of the universe, whose Power was sent forth through space in the form of a Thought and then as a Word; not a simple word, but the Creative Fiat, which scientific observations describe as Cosmic Waves. This Creative Fiat, by its sounding vibrations marshaled the millions of chaotic atoms into many shapes and forms, from starfish to star, from microbe to humans; in fact, all things that constitute and inhabit the universe. The syllables and sounds of this Creative Word are being sent forth, one after another through the ages. They create new species and evolve the older ones. All this goes on according to the Archetype and plan conceived in the Great Architect's Mind before the dynamic force of the Creative Word was sent out into the abyss of space. God, or the Great Intelligence which the Universe is the physical manifestation, is the source of all things. It is in this Force that we really, truly, and literally live and move, and have our being. The Psalmist [6] expresses this truth when he says:

Where can I go from Your Spirit?
Or where can I flee from Your presence?
If I ascend into heaven, You are there;
If I make my bed in hell, behold, You are there.
If I take the wings of the morning,
And dwell in the uttermost parts of the sea,
Even there Your hand shall lead me,
And Your right hand shall hold me.

The above described creative process applies to our human creative faculties as well. When a person desires to create something, s/he first makes him/herself familiar with the subject-matter of his/her interest. As s/he visualizes his/her creation, s/he frames the idea in time and space, fills it with his/her whole being, permeating every atom of the root-substance of that concept with his/her life, as to awaken the activity latent within every integrated part of the concept. When s/he has thus prepared the

---

[6] Psalm 139:7-12

material for his/her invention, s/he next sets it in order. The root-substance is set in varying rates of functionality and is therefore differently constituted in its various divisions and functions. Every part of the system is pervaded by the inventor's thought power so that a change or modification in the original thought would impact each part of the division. This root-substance becomes an expression of the negative pole of the thought of the Thinker, or output, while the thought itself is an expression of the positive energy of the inventor, or input. From the work of one upon the other, the invention can become Real.

It is, however, important to point out that though in the alphabet we have a few elementary sounds from which words may be constructed and that are basic elements of expression in music, literature, or poetry; and though bricks, iron, and lumber are raw materials of architecture, a heap of bricks, iron, and lumber, is not a house, nor is a jumbled mass of notes music, neither can we call a haphazard arrangement of alphabetical sounds a word. These raw materials are prime necessities in the construction of architecture, music, literature, or poetry, but the contour of the finished product and the purpose it will serve depend upon the arrangement of the raw materials, which is subject to the constructor's design and objectives. In this respect, building materials may be formed into prison or palace; notes may be arranged as fanfare or funeral dirge; words may be indicted to inspire passion or peace, all according to the will of the designer.

As said earlier, our destiny as humanity is to become dynamic creators. We have the capability of thinking, we may voice our thoughts with words, and where we are not capable of carrying out our ideas alone, we may secure the help of others to realize them. Moreover, a time will come when we will create directly by the Word of our mouth, so that when in time we become able to use our Word to create directly we will know how. At the present time, however, we would make many mistakes with such power. Besides, we are not yet good of heart and our thoughts are mostly selfish so that we would bring into being monstrous creations in the likeness of our own thoughts, feelings, and words.

This process is nevertheless unstoppable. For example, in our earliest dawn endeavor as humanity, we only worked on and used the SOLID to express our creative nature; muscular force was our only means of performing work, and from bones and stones that we picked up from the ground, we shaped our first crude instruments to be wielded by our arm. Then came a time when in a rude dug-out we first trusted ourselves to the waters; a LIQUID and the water wheel was the first machinery. The liquid is already much stronger than the solid. A wave will raze the decks of a ship, tear out masts and twist the stoutest iron bar as if it were a thin wire. But water power is a stationary force and therefore limited to work in its immediate vicinity. When we learned to use the still more subtle force which we call AIR, it became possible for us to erect windmills in any place to do the work and sailing vessels brought the whole world into interconnection, communication, and cooperation. Thus, our next step in unfoldment was achieved by the use of Wind, a force still subtler than water and more universally applicable than that element. But wind was fickle and not to be depended upon. Therefore, the advancement in human civilization achieved by its use paled into insignificance when we discovered how to utilize the still more subtle gas, which is called STEAM.

With this new force, we made enormous progress in our lifestyle and improved previously made progress. There was, however, the drawback to the use of and the utility of steam-power, in that it required cumbersome transmission machinery. This drawback was eventually and practically eliminated by the discovery and the application of a still subtler invisible and intangible force, more readily transmissible; ELECTRICITY. But that was not the last word on the human ingenuity. The invention of the ELECTRONIC has brought the world development to a level unimagined before. The use of computers and internet cannot be understated as it has revolutionized almost all aspects of our life. Yet, we are still far from averaging the creative capacities latent in us, but which we will display and use effectively in the future.

This shows us that human progress in the past has depended upon the utilization of forces of increasing subtlety, each force in the scale being more capable of transmission than the ones previously available. From this fact we can readily realize that further progress depends upon the discovery of still finer forces transmissible with still greater facility. We know for example that the force we now call Digital Wireless Transmission is accomplished without the use of wires, but even this system is not ideal; it is very much dependent upon energy generated both from electricity and in a central data server, which in a large part is stationary. It also involves the use of complicated and costly machinery, and is, therefore, out of reach for many people. Moreover, its infrastructure is vulnerable to hazardous events as well as to malicious activities such as hacking, cyber criminality, and eventually cyber war. The ideal force, therefore, would be a power which we could generate from ourselves at any moment without machinery. This is the force of the future, which is latent within every one of us and which we speak of sometimes as EMOTION.

We feel its far-reaching power at times as temper when it is unleashed, and we say that "a person has lost control of him/herself." No amount of work can so tire the physical body and wreck it as when the enormous energy of EMOTIONS is let loose in a fit of temper. At our present stage of evolution, this enormous force sleeps, and it is well that it should be so until we have learned to follow the directives of the Inner Power and the use of our Thought Power, which is a still more subtle force. This world is a school to teach us how to use these two subtle forces; that is, the power of thought and the power of emotion. Just as we are mastering the digital world by creating digital things we can share digitally with others; the time will soon come when we will be able to use the power of our Thought and Word to create real things and apply the power of Emotion to transmit these creations to others in ways much faster and safer than Internet.

The future is unknown to us and whatever prediction on our potential powers may sound like a fetch fetching fiction. But, the Powers of Thought, Word, and Emotion are upon and within us. If we consider the wonderful power of the human Word in our daily lives, we know that coming to us in the sweet accents of love, words may lure us from paths of rectitude to shameful ignominy and wreck our life with sorrow and remorse, or it may spur us on in noblest efforts to acquire glory and honor, here or hereafter. According to the inflection of the voice, a word may strike terror into the bravest heart or lull a timid child to peaceful slumber. The word of an agitator may rouse the passions of a mob and impel it to awful bloodshed. The grim memories of the holocaust, genocides, and many mass killings and destructions of cities, villages, and societies, where dictatorial mandates of mob-rule killed and exiled at pleasure are a reminder of what human words can do. On the other hand, the strain of "Home, Sweet Home" may cement the setting of a family-circle beyond possibility of rupture. Right words are true and therefore free; they are never bound or fettered by time or space; they go to farthest corners of earth, and when the lips that spoke them first have long since moldered in the grave, other voices take up their message of life and love with unshakable enthusiasm, as illustrated by Beethoven's ODE OF JOY, which strikes the feeling of universal unity even in hearts totally removed from such aspiration. Words of peace have been victorious where war would have meant defeat, and no talent is more to be desired than the ability to always say the right word at the auspicious time.

Considering thus the immense power and potency of the human word, we may perhaps dimly apprehend the potential magnitude of the Word of God, the Creative Fiat, when, as a mighty dynamic force, it first reverberated through space and commenced to form the primordial matter into solar systems, galaxies, planets, and billions of beings that inhabit them, as a sound from a violin bow molds sand into geometrical figures. Moreover, the Cosmic Logos continues to sustain the marching orbs of the stars and impel them onwards in their circle paths; the Creative Word continues to produce forms of gradually increasing efficiency as media expressing life and consciousness. The harmonious enunciation of consecutive syllables in the Divine Creative Word build successive stages in the evolution of the universe and in humans. When the last syllable has been spoken and the complete word has sounded, we shall have reached perfection as human beings. Should this Sound stop vibrating in the Cosmic Matter, on the other hand, all that exists would suddenly stop.

Thought is undoubtedly the most powerful means of obtaining knowledge. If it is concentrated upon a subject, as will be discussed, it will burn its way through any obstacle and solve the problem. If the requisite amount of Thought Force is brought to bear, there is nothing that is beyond the power of human comprehension. Many of us have formed the habit of listless thinking, which makes us incapable of holding onto any subject until it is thoroughly mastered. Although thoughts, which flit through the mind may be good, bad, or indifferent - mostly the latter - the mind does not usually hold on to any one of them sufficiently long to learn its nature. Thought-control is often very difficult to achieve. But, once attained, however, the possessor of such thought-control can hold within his/her hand the key to success in whatever line s/he may be engaged. So long as we scatter this treasure, Thought Force is of little use to us, but as soon as we are prepared to undertake the trouble necessary to harness it, all knowledge is ours. Consequently, since Thought is our principal power, we must learn how to have absolute control of it, so that what we produce is not illusion induced by outside conditions, but true imagination generated by the Inner Power, or the God within. As discussed in the next chapter, thought-control skills can be developed by performing the daily exercise of Concentration, regularly and with persistence. This can be achieved by learning how to fix the minds unwaveringly upon a single subject, by becoming so absorbed in it that all else is successfully blotted out of consciousness. Once we have learned to do this, we can become able to see the many sides of things or ideas illuminated by the light of the Inner Power, and thus obtain knowledge of the inner nature of things and ideas undreamed of before.

We speak of Thought as being conceived by the mind, but just as both a male and a female are necessary in the generation of an offspring, so also are both idea and mind necessary before a thought can be conceived. An idea is generated by our Inner Power, or Inner God; COGITO ERGO SUM - I think, therefore I AM. This idea is projected upon the receptive mind, giving birth to a thought. So, when each idea clothes itself in a form made of mind-stuff, it is then a thought, as visible to the inner vision of its author just as a child is to his/her parents. Thus, we see that ideas are embryonic thoughts, nuclei of root-substance from the inner worlds. Improperly conceived in an adversely affected mind, they become vagaries and delusions, but when gestated in a sane mind and formed into rational thoughts they are the basis of all material, moral, and mental progress. At the present time, however, our mind is not focused in a way that enables it to give a clear and true picture of what the Inner God imagines. It is not one-pointed, and it gives misty and clouded pictures. Hence, the necessity of experiment to show the inadequacy of first conception, and of bringing about new imaginings and ideas until the image produced in the mental substance has been reproduced in physical substance. Our existence in the physical and concrete realm is constantly compelling us to learn how to think aright and develop our epigenesis in constructive ways.

To illustrate the above assertion, let us take the

example of an inventor who gets an idea of a device that can solve a given world pressing problem. The idea is not yet a thought; it is a sudden insight, a message from the Inner Power recorded on the mind, that has not yet taken shape. Gradually, however, the inventor visualizes it in his/her mind. S/he forms a device in his/her thought, and before his/her mental vision that device appears with all its functions operating as necessary to accomplish the required work. Then s/he begins to draw the plans for the device; but wait! It appears that even at this stage modifications are necessary. Thus, we see that already the physical conditions show the inventor where his/her thought was not correct. Even after building the device with appropriate materials, more modifications usually are necessary. Perhaps s/he may have to discard the first model and build an entirely different one. As s/he progresses, the concrete physical conditions have enabled him/her to detect the flaw in his/her reasoning; they force him/her to make the necessary modifications in the original thought to bring out a device that will do the work.

The same principle holds good in business, philanthropy, or in politics. If our thoughts concerning the various matters in life are wrong, they are corrected when brought into practical use. Therefore, when we make errors and mistakes, we should never get depressed by thinking that things should always be perfect at the first attempt, or the second, or the third, for we are constantly being reminded that we have a huge room for improvement. Mistake is never an option, because it is part of the process that eventually can lead to success. It is wonderful and necessary that we dwell in this physical world and learn to wield the Power of Thought; a power being, at the present times, held in check to a great extent by our material conditions.

From a different token, we sometimes argue that we have the right to think what we want, and that wicked thoughts, if not translated into wicked deeds, are not harmful. This is far from true, and the power of wicked thoughts, just as the power of good and beneficent ones, is great indeed. Through the course of centuries, for instance, human's evil thoughts of fear and hatred have been vanquished by the opposite force; courage. When a contagious disease is approached with fear and trembling, the poisonous microbes tend to spread at a fast pace to become a pandemic. If, on the other hand, we handle the disease in a perfectly fearless attitude, we fight back and find remedies and cures to the pandemic. Similarly, when we realize that "as we think in our heart, so are we," we shall have a much clearer conception of life than we do if we take into consideration only individual specific acts. Indeed, every act is the outcome of a previous thought, but not necessarily the thought of the person committing the act. If a tuning fork is struck and another tuning fork of the same pitch is in the vicinity, as previously mentioned, the second one will ring in concert with the first.

Likewise, when we think a thought and another person in our environment has been thinking along the same line, our thoughts coalesce with his/hers and strengthen that person for good or evil, according to the nature of the thought. Have you ever found yourself in a situation where you are thinking of a certain song in your head just to hear your neighbor singing it loud? Indeed, if we have been in the habit of thinking evil, malicious thoughts against someone, these thoughts may have been attractive to that person. On the principle that a saturated solution of salt will require only a single crystal to make it solidify, so also, if we have saturated our mind with thoughts of murder for example, the thought of murder that another person sends out may prove to be the last straw to destroy that last barrier, which would have kept a murderer from committing an evil act. Therefore, our thoughts are of vastly more importance than our acts. If we always think right, we shall always act right. In fact, no person can think to loving someone, no person can scheme about how to help someone emotionally, mentally, or physically without also acting out these thoughts. If we cultivate such thoughts, we shall soon find sunshine spreading around us; we shall find that people will meet us in the same spirit that we send out. If we generate a serene attitude and thoughts that are free from covetousness and are frankly honest and helpful, we shall call out the best in other people. Therefore, let us realize that it is not until we have cultivated the better qualities in ourselves that we can expect to find them in others. We are thus most certainly responsible for our thoughts. If we want to obtain help to cultivate better qualities, then let us seek the company of people who are already good, for their attitude of mind will be of immense help to us in calling forth our own finer qualities.

Generally, it does not always appear easy to rid ourselves of evil thoughts, and most of us cannot help but encounter people or situations which call forth negative thinking, try as we will to fight it. But there is a simpler way of dismissing such unwanted thoughts which does not involve "fighting them" at all.

To arrive at a correct understanding of how thoughts of good or bad attract their likeness, it is necessary to realize that our thoughts are intrinsically connected to and are often influenced by our feelings, desires, and emotions. These are all under the domination of two great forces: **Attraction** and **Repulsion**. The tendency of every thought, desire, or emotion is to attract itself all it can of a like nature and grow thereby - *the likes attract the likes*! If the force of attraction governs the realm of good thoughts, desires, and emotions, these will create snowball effect and amalgamate to bring joy, love, peace, and constructive undertakings in our lives and in this world. If, on the other hand, this tendency to attraction were to predominate in bad thoughts and desires, evil would grow like a weed in our world. There would be anarchy instead of order in the Cosmos. This, fortunately, is prevented by the preponderating power of the force of Repulsion in the realm of bad thoughts, desires, and emotions. As a result of this predominance, when for example a coarse desire or thought form is being attracted to another of the same nature, there is a disharmony in their vibrations, whereby one has a disintegrating effect upon the other. Thus, instead of uniting and amalgamating evil with evil, they act with mutual destructiveness and in that way the evil in the world is kept within reasonable bounds.

When we understand how the twin forces of Attraction and Repulsion work in this respect, we are in a position to understand that anything happening in the Physical World is also reflected in and by our thoughts and builds its appropriate form in our emotions. When, for example, a true account of a situation is given, another form is built, exactly like the first. The force of Attraction then draws them together and they coalesce, strengthening each other. If, on the other hand, an untrue recount is given, a form different from and antagonistic to the first, or true one, is created. As they deal with the same occurrence, they are drawn together by the law of attraction, but because their vibrations are different, the force of repulsion causes them to act upon each other with mutual destructiveness. Therefore, if untrue accounts are strong enough and repeated often enough, evil and malicious lies can kill anything that is good. Conversely, seeking for the good in evil will, in time, transmute the evil into good. If the thought form that is built to minimize the evil is weak, it will have no effect and will be destroyed by the evil form; but if it is strong and frequently repeated, it will have the effect of disintegrating the evil and substituting the good. That effect, be it distinctly understood, is not brought about by lying, nor denying the evil, but by looking for the good. This is why it is important that we practice this principle of looking for good in all things very rigidly, because we know what a power it possesses in keeping down evil.

But whether an object or an idea we are dealing with is good and attractive or bad and repulsive is not in itself important. It is rather our feeling, whether of **Interest** or **Indifference** that is the determining factor as to the fate of the object or idea. Interest in or indifference to an object or an idea sways the balance in favor of one of Attraction or Repulsion forces, thereby relegating the object or idea as good or bad. If Interest (meaning we are interested) is the feeling with which we meet an impression of an object or an idea, it has the same effect upon that impression as sunlight and air have upon a plant. That idea will grow and flourish in our mind and life. If, on the other hand, we meet an impression or idea with Indifference, it withers as does a plant when put in a dark cellar. Thus, from our feeling for an object or an idea, or a person come the incentive to action, or the decision to refrain there from, for these twin feelings of Interest and Indifference furnish the incentive to action and are the springs that move the world. It is however aspirational that the determining factor for our action or inaction be *duty and service,* but especially service, because when guided by love and rendered with self-forgetting intent, it becomes *the "Mysterium Magnum";* the fastest, the safest, and the most joyful road to God. Self-forgetting service is therefore the formula to Greatness in the sanctuary of the Inner God!

So, when we are interested in an object, idea, or a person, the feeling of Interest can start either the force of Attraction or Repulsion for that object, idea, or person. If, on the contrary, we show Indifference, this feeling will simply have a withering effect on the object or idea against which it is directed, so far as our connection with it is concerned. Indifference, however, can be deemed passive action in cases where interest and action are the only expected responses to a dire situation. In the same line, if our interest in a person, an object, or an idea generates

Repulsion, that naturally causes us to expurgate from our lives any connection with the person, object, or idea which roused it; but there is a great difference between the action of the force of Repulsion and the mere feeling of Indifference. Perhaps an illustration will make illuminate the operation of the twin Feelings and the twin Forces.

Three friends are watching the news on TV. They see a scene of a war devastated city with many malnourished children; the kids are visibly sick, skinny, many with openly wounded limbs, and evidently suffering intensely from famine and diseases. This much is evident to all three friends - their senses tell them that. Now come the feelings; two of the friends take an "interest" in the children, but in the third there is a feeling of "indifference." S/he passes on, turning his/her attention to the food being delivered instead. The others remain focused on the news; they are both interested, but each of them manifests interest in quite different ways. The interest of one is sympathetic and helpful, impelling her/him to think about how to care for the poor children, to end war and bring back peace and health to the city. In her/him the feeling of interest has aroused the force of Attraction. The other friend's interest is rather of a different kind. S/he sees only a loathsome sight which is revolting to her/him and wishes to rid her/himself and the world of such depressing scenes as quickly as possible. S/he even goes as far as expressing the wish that the city and its inhabitants should be ripped off the world map. In her/him the feeling of interest generates the destructive force of Repulsion.

Finally, the feeling of Interest can arouse the force of Attraction and be directed toward things, thoughts, desires, and people who are bad in their nature. As said early, Attraction dominates in the realm of good, but it also operates in both realms of good and evil. Repulsion, on the other hand, only operates and predominates in bad. Unfortunately, the history of humankind is full of examples of how the force of Repulsion can be recklessly activated with the only purpose of destroying good, beauty, and truth, or just for inflicting grief and suffering to others as well as to ourselves. For this reason, love, friendship, and many beautiful things are often mingled with grief! What can happen in these cases is a real ravel of human conscience. From the battle of the twin forces of Attraction and Repulsion results all the pain and suffering incident to wrongdoing or misdirected effort, whether intentional or otherwise. Thus, we can see how important the feeling we have concerning anything is, for upon that depends the nature of the atmosphere we create for ourselves. If we love the good, we shall keep and nourish as guardian angels all that is good about us; if it is the reverse, we can be ensured that we are populating our path with demons of our own breeding.

In sum, both like and dislike tend to attract a thought or an idea to us, and the added thought force we send out to fight evil thoughts will keep them alive and bring them to our mind oftener, in the same way that quarreling may cause a person we dislike waylaying us for spite. Instead of fighting, let us adopt the tactic of indifference. If we turn our heads the other way when we meet a person we dislike, s/he will soon grow tired of following us. On the same principle, if we but turn away with indifference when thoughts of evil come into our minds, and apply our minds to something that is good and ideal, then we shall find in a short time that we are rid of the evil thoughts and have only the good thoughts we desire to entertain, for:

"With reason's torch we search for truth
To restore the harmony, life, and youth;
For reason's torch when thus applied

In wisdom's quest is safest guide.
If we persist' though oft we fail,
In time our efforts shall prevail
To end the discord and dispel
All evil with harmony's rhythmic swell."

The power of thought, as said earlier, is one of the strongest forces known to us and is far-reaching. All things, whether for good or ill, can be accomplished with it. Only when we come to an understanding of the true nature and proper use of this force, can we free ourselves from the fetters of failure, suffering, and sorrow, and continue the upward path towards becoming self-conscious Creative Beings. This is the Quest we must undertake, which is also the center of this discussion. As elaborated in the next chapter, we can learn how to gain control of our Thought Power by harnessing the use of Concentration, Meditation, and Prayer. By making a conscious and volitional effort to practice these exercises, we allow ourselves to communicate with our Inner Power, which allows us to rise above mere material consideration, to realize the timelessness of all Good, and to find that vital spark of the Divine, which is enfolded in every human being. These exercises are our gears for the Quest.

Chapter 3
Gearing up for the Quest

The nature and the necessity of life have given us important Gears to use in our Daily Quest. These same tools are channels we can use to increase our ability to communicate with the Inner Power and gain control of our Thought Power. They are also mechanisms through which we can conquer a sound body, a sane mind, and a soft heart, for the more we use them, the sharper and easy to use they become. These tools are the exercises of Concentration, Meditation, and Prayer.

1. **Concentration**

Concentration is a word that puzzles many and carries meaning to but few, and is often confused with Meditation. The dictionary gives several definitions, all applicable to this essay. One is "to draw to a center," another one from chemistry, it means "to reduce to extreme purity and strength by removing valueless constituents." From Latin *com* "with, together" and *centrum* "center", the verb to

concentrate means to bring or come to a common center".
In this sense, the word Concentration conveys the meaning
of "focus".

Applied to our discussion, one of the above definitions
tells us that if we draw our thoughts to a center, to a point,
we increase their strength on the principle that the power
of the sun's rays is increased when focused to a point by
means of a magnifying glass. In the same line, and to
borrow from chemistry, by eliminating from our mind for
the time being all other subjects, our whole thought power
is available for use in attaining an object or solving the
problem on which we are concentrating. During
concentration, one may become so absorbed in a subject
that if a cannon were fired above his/her heads s/he would
not hear it. We may recall times when we happened to be
so lost in a book that we were oblivious to all else.
Therefore, for us to harness the Power of Thought, we
must develop the ability of becoming equally absorbed in
the idea we are concentrating upon, so that we may shut
out the world of sense from our consciousness and give
our full attention to the task. When we learn to do that, we
will see the invisible side of an object or of an idea
illuminated by the inner light, and thus we will obtain a

knowledge of the inner nature of things or ideas we are concentrating on.

A] Practicing Concentration

First and foremost, we must remember that Thought Force is our principal individual power and the most powerful mean of obtaining knowledge. As previously mentioned, our task is to learn how to control this immense power. The exercise of Concentration is one of the tools we have as we learn to gain thought control. It is very important that we gain such control, because without it the power flows aimlessly, accomplishing nothing.

To learn the art of concentration, the first thing to practice is fixing our thought upon some ideal and holding it there without letting it swerve. This may be an exceedingly hard task at the start, but to some extent at least, it must be accomplished before it is possible to make any further progress. As previously mentioned, thought is the power we use in making images, pictures, or thought forms, according to ideas from within. Every attempt to concentrate is a good direction and will have its value. When we have learned to concentrate on one thing to the exclusion of all other things, we will progressively increase our Thought Power, gain the ability to use it effectively, and the control of it. We also attain quality by diminishing the often-excessive quantity.

Skeptics may argue that it is *all* imagination. But, as said before, if inventors had not been able to imagine the telephone, machines, software, etc., we would not today possess those things. Also, inventors' imaginings were not generally correct or true at first, otherwise the inventions would have worked successfully from the beginning, without the many failures and apparently useless experiments that have nearly always preceded the production of the practical and serviceable enterprises, tools, or machines. Neither is the imagination of a budding apprentice correct at first. The only way to make it true is by uninterrupted practice, day after day, exercising the will to keep the thought focused upon one subject, object, or idea, exclusive all else.

It is true to say that thought is a great power we have been accustomed to waste. It has been allowed to flow on aimlessly, as water flows over a precipice before it is captured and directed to the reservoir. We often hear people exclaim petulantly: "oh, I cannot think of a hundred things at once!" In fact, that's exactly what we have been doing, and what has caused the very trouble of which we complain; that is, having trouble concentrating our thought. We are constantly thinking of a hundred things other than the one we have at hand. Every success, however, has been accomplished by persistent concentration upon the desired end. But, just as the rays of the Sun, diffused over the entire surface of the Earth, produce only a moderate warmth, if even a few of the rays are concentrated by means of a glass, they can produce fire at the focusing point, so is our thought when focused on one point.

This is something anyone who wants to harness the Power of Thought must positively learn to do. There is no other way. At first, we will find ourselves thinking of everything under the sun instead of the problem we need to solve, the solution we may be exploring, or the ideal upon which we have decided to concentrate. But we must not let that discourage us. In time we will find it easier to still our senses and hold our thoughts steady. Persistence, *persistence*, and always *persistence* will win at last. Without that, however, no results can be expected. Moreover, it is of no use to practice concentration for two or three mornings or weeks and then neglect exercising for as long. But just as we need to follow through with the workout before we can enjoy the benefit in our physical shape, endurance, and comfort, to be effective concentration exercise must be done faithfully every day until out mind is trained to pick it up at any moment. When we have reached that point of abstraction, the sense centers of our feelings and emotions commence to revolve slowly within the physical body as we become used to the practice. Just as we train our physical muscles by using them and just as we feel soreness first before becoming comfortable with the exercise, in time our power of concentration will become more and more defined and it will require less and less effort to get it going.

B] The subject of concentration

The subject of Concentration exercise may be any high and lofty ideal, quote, or a symbol. The object matters little, but whatever it is we must imagine it true to life in all details. What matters in this respect is that the object of concentration should preferably be of such a nature that it takes us out of the ordinary things of sense, beyond time and space. Any subject may be selected, according to each individual temperament and mental persuasion, so long as it is pure and mentally uplifting in its tendency. Someone may choose a spark of light in a dark room and concentrate on it; those who love flowers, buildings, machinery, or art would be most easily helped by taking one of their affections as the subject of concentration. If it is the Sun, we must imagine a real Sun, with mobile features, shining, vibrating, and giving life to billions of beings in the universe, and an expression that is not stony and dead. For those who follow the biblical scriptures for example, there is no better formula than the first five verses of St. John's gospel previously mentioned. Taking them as subject, sentence by sentence, morning after morning, will in time give them a wonderful insight into the genesis of our universe. But it is important that during Concentration we visualize our target in such clear and complete outlines, for only then we can enter the spirit of concentration. There must be no shadowy imaging, or faint resemblance. Obviously, at first the pictures on which we concentrate will be but shadowy and poor likenesses, but in the end we can, with consistent exercise, conjure up an image more real and alive than things in the physical world.

When we have become able to form such pictures and have succeeded in holding our mind upon them, we may try to drop the picture suddenly and, holding the mind steady without any thought, wait to see what comes into the vacuum. We may then be surprisingly delighted with sights and scenes of the inner world filling the vacant space. At that point, we may switch our focus on this or that subject, idea, or problem, investigate them and obtain the answers that we seek.

C] When to practice

After realizing the value of the art of Concentration, we will be eager to practice it daily. We can take advantage of the time we spend on recess, public transportation, airport while waiting for a flight, or in similar places where the mind has a chance to wander and concentrate it on an object or an ideal. It only takes a few minutes to try.

Many of us have been told that the quiet of a monastery, the isolation in the wood, the peacefulness of the mountain cabin, etc....are the best conditions to practice concentration, meditation, and prayer; that the noisy public transportation, the ambient crack of machinery, the back and forth at the factory, the screams of children on the school playground, the deafening sounds of explosion in the war zone, or many other places filled with crowding distractions would not seem to be the best places to practice concentration. This is perhaps true for the first days in the practice, but if we can learn better under such adverse conditions, then, having succeeded under difficulties, we will always find it easier to gather our thoughts into single-pointedness when we have the chance for quiet concentration. As a rule, our minds do not hold any one thought long enough to penetrate its nature and complete meaning. To gain control of our thought is a great achievement; and anyone who has mastered this difficult accomplishment has the key to success in any field at his/her command. Once again, every attempt has its value; the only failure is when we stop trying. And, as Nelson Mandela once said, "a saint is a sinner who dies trying to do good".

As a result of our ability to concentrate, we not only gain in clarity of our thoughts, this clarity will rid us of confusion and frustration caused by shadowy thoughts, which often contribute to our physical discomfort, but we will also gain control of our thought in the proportion of our ability to do so. Such control enables us to gain mastery of our desires, feelings, and especially emotions, which as pointed out earlier, is our future force of information transmission. In this respect, and as discussed in the section on Prayer, it is worth mentioning that the destructive desires and emotions such as anger, hate, revenge, resentment, but particularly anger, disrupt and disarrange the thought forms and the thought creations of good we may have previously made, and thereby delay their materialization. When we have yielded to anger or revenge, for instance, and dissipated some mental creation of good, the corresponding thought form configuration must reassemble itself before materialization can proceed. This takes time and delays the time frame when there might have been a favorable change in our environment or general fortune. Therefore, we see the great importance of keeping our feelings and emotions under check. But, the most important benefit of concentration is that we eventually become more receptive to the directives from our Inner Power.

A question may be asked: "How can we avoid harmful thoughts and desires, and keep them out of our mind? It seems almost impossible at time to keep them from slipping in." The answer is *thought substitution*. It is based on the principle that two thoughts cannot occupy the mind at the same time and is similar to the principle of physics that two bodies cannot occupy the same space at the same time. When we are bothered by harmful thoughts of any kind, it is well to *substitute another thought* and concentrate on it so positively that the harmful thought cannot get in. This answer is very simple and only requires practice to make it comparatively easy. Harmful desires are excluded from the mind by the same process. Thus, by substituting some constructive thought in place of the thought of wrong desire, the latter is very nearly shut out.

Lastly, one of the abilities everyone would wish to develop through concentration is the power to heal illness, to build a sound body, a soft heart, and a sane mind. Such power implies that we become able to direct our thought power inside our physical and to control our body systems' activities at will, which we are incapable of doing at our current stage of evolution. Our physical body is a marvel. The perfection of construction and intelligent adaptability displayed in this instrument reflect the work of a genius. Yet, we are to a large extent ignorant or unaware of how it works and why it gets sick and dies. Medical sciences teach us that our vital system, for example, is designed around two of the body's main systems: the cardiovascular system and the respiratory system. That the heart is the most important muscle in the body and its function is essential for life. It works as a pulsatile, four-chamber pump that moves the blood around the body. That lungs are a key part of the respiratory system which provides oxygen to the body. That lymphatic system plays an important role in circulation by draining fluids that accumulate in the extracellular space during capillary exchange and returning them to the blood. It also helps in defense against bad bacteria, pathogens, viruses, and cancerous tumors as well as in transporting fats. But the point being made here is that all this amazingly organized system and many other vital functions pertaining to our physiology and anatomy occur inside our body without our conscious participation.

The area of gastronomy can serve as another example. It is generally known, in a vague kind of way, that the gastric juice acts upon the food to promote assimilation. But, only a very few people, outside of the medical profession, are aware that there are many different gastric juices, each appropriate to the treatment of a certain kind of food. The researches of Pavlov, however, have established the fact beyond doubt that there is one kind of juice for the digestion of meat, another for milk, another for acid fruit, etc. That fact, by the way, is the reason why all foods do not mix well ([7]). When the finding of the gastric juices' selection was first proven, scientists were sorely puzzled trying to learn how the right kind of juice

---

[7] https://www.nobelprize.org/prizes/medicine/1904/pavlov/lecture/

was selected and caused to enter the stomach *before* the food. They thought the signal was given along the nervous system. But the work of Starling and Bayliss demonstrated that the proper juice was poured into the stomach even though the nervous system was blocked ([8]). In fact, in a series of experiments of brilliant ingenuity, these two scientists proved that infinitesimal parts of food are taken up by the blood as soon as the food enters the mouth, go in advance to the digestive glands and cause a flow of the proper juice. But again, we do not consciously participate or direct the processes and functions as to how these juices are selected inside our stomach, nor do we even have an idea of the metabolism through which they combine and are distributed in the system. Let's agree that everyone would like to have the power to control the above functions and have a say in what is happening inside our bodies.

We all have experienced and do experience illness, disease, and discomfort in our body. The matter of fact is that we are not aware of many of the internal organs of our bodies and we are not conscious of how they function to

---

[8] https://www.ncbi.nlm.nih.gov/pmc/articles/PMC1665254/

sustain our lives. The only time we become aware of them is when these organs are defective, when they are under attack from pathogens, or when they start to malfunction. We all agree that it can be understandably very frustrating to feel trapped, powerless, and incapable to direct the flow of the vital fuel inside our body. No matter how strong our will power can be, no matter how powerful our brain is, and no matter how strong our prayers can be, we are incapable of handling the flux and reflux of the vital energy inside our bodies. When we are finally overcome by the sting of illness, we eventually entrust the management of our health to medical professionals, all of whom are not immune from the same limitations.

What is more frustrating is that during certain protracted illnesses, we become so intent upon the suffering that we powerlessly and passively watch our system ceasing to fully vivify the cells. Thus, bodily ailment breeds mental inaction and it becomes almost impossible to throw off disease without a special impulse to dispel the mental fog and start the cell activities anew. In the attempt to recover from illness, we either undergo medical procedures, or are prescribed medication, or both. With medications specifically, medical sciences teach us that when we take them by mouth, in pill, capsule, or liquid form, they are swallowed and pass into the digestive system. They are then broken down in either the stomach or the intestines and are absorbed in the same way as food. They then pass through the liver before entering the bloodstream. Once a medication enters the bloodstream, it circulates to the site where its action is needed. However, like in the case of gastric juices, assimilation or repulsion of medication inside our body operates with neither our conscious knowledge nor contribution as to where to direct good stuff and expel unnecessary chemicals, nor do we volitionally direct the quantity and the manner in which the bloodstream should flow inside our system. In situations such as these, we intensively but vainly wish we could control the course of the events happening inside our body. We wish to have the power to control the bloodstream in our veins! Such power we indeed have, though we have not yet learned the knowledge, skills, and ability to use it.

The blood is the highest expression of life in our body, for it nourishes the entire physical organism. In this sense, the blood is the fuel of the Inner Power. Without blood, our Inner Power can neither guide and control its dense instrument, nor use it as electric energy to act on the nervous system. It makes perfect sense that we all desire the power to decide where to concentrate our bloodstream and drive it to wherever we unfold the greatest activity at any time. Wouldn't it be wonderful that if a situation requires sudden thought and action, we had the power to prompt the blood drive to the head? Or if a heavy meal is to be digested to send the greater portion of the blood from the head to be centered around the digestive organs? Or if we feel sick and discomfort to direct the bloodstream to the part of the body so affected and speed restoration and recovery? All these examples are meant to show that during the waking hours, the Inner Power works in and controls the dense body by means of the blood. The larger portion of the total amount goes to that part of the body where at any given time the Inner Power unfolds any particular activity. However, at this stage of our life, our conscious mind is unaware and not volitionally involved in such operations. As matter of fact, there is in every little cell of the human body a separate cell life, but over and above that, and as we now know, there is the Inner God, the I AM, who directs and controls all cells so that they act in harmony, just as the Great ArchiTekton, the God of the universe directs and controls all things.

Our Daily Quest is to learn how to enable our conscious mind to align with the Inner Power so that in time we may conquer the power to willingly and consciously control all the anatomical and biological vital operations of our body in the same way we currently, though to a limited extent, commend our voluntary muscles.

In this regard, medical sciences teach us of two kinds of muscles: voluntary and involuntary. ([9]) Voluntary muscles are those that are controlled by *will* through the voluntary nervous system, such as the muscles of the hand and arm. They are striped both lengthwise and crosswise. Involuntary muscles, on the other hand, are formed in lengthwise stripes only and relate to functions not under the control of the will, such as digestion, breathing, assimilation, excretion, circulation, etc.

Ordinarily, as already pointed out, we cannot control the circulation of blood in our veins, the digestion of foods, or the beating of our heart, and many other vital functions. But there is something of utmost importance happening in our system; some sort of puzzle, which once solved can be

---

[9] https://biologydictionary.net/muscular-system/

the key to our emancipation from the restrictions we now face with respect to the control of our physical and vital systems. As previously mentioned, our heart is the most important muscle in the body and its function is essential for our physical body to stay alive. Under normal conditions, the heart-beat for example is a fixed quantity, which makes it impossible to control because the heart is an involuntary muscle. Yet, to the bewilderment of physiologists and medical experts, the heart is *cross*-striped like a voluntary muscle. ([10]) It is the only organ in the body exhibiting this peculiarity. But, sphinxlike, it refuses to give scientists an answer to the riddle. This anomaly, however, can be deemed a promising benefit, because it indicates that in a possible future, which we can only think of in terms of fiction at this time, when our conscious mind will have learned to fully follow the directives of the Inner Power, we could gain more and more control over the heart, the cross-stripes would gradually develop to transform the heart into a voluntary muscle, so that we could use it in the same way we are currently using all other cross-stripped voluntary muscles. Moreover, as will be

---

[10] https://biologydictionary.net/cardiac-muscle/

discussed in the next section, when the blood passes through the heart, cycle after cycle, hour after hour all through our life, it engraves the pictures of our conscious or unconscious interactions with the outside world and observed through senses, and carries upon both our conscious and subconscious memories, while they are still fresh, thus making a faithful record of our life experience. These records are a trove of treasures we should be able to access and learn from. However, for obvious reasons, we are barred from accessing this jewel on the same premises that a young heir or heiress is restricted from managing his/her inheritance and until s/he is capable and matures enough to assume responsibilities and functions associated with the management of such assets. Similarly, the time will come when, after developing the abilities to concentrate and control our Thought Power, we will develop and use the power to decide how, when, and where to deploy it both inside and outside our bodies. Such abilities will, among many competencies, give us the power to control the functions of our heart and the flow of the blood supply in our body and direct it wherever the activities inside the body need it the most. Such control will allow us the power to restore health; that is, to build up the areas of our cells destroyed by mental, emotional, physical activities, and diseases. Such power, however, can only be conquered by emancipating our mind from the domination of self-serving desires, fear, hatred, and anger. Most importantly, we must free our mind from ignorance, the only sin; applied knowledge being salvation.

Finally, we all at times have the urgent need to send helpful thoughts to others. However, no matter how great our wish to comply may be, only the concentrated thoughts have the strength to arrive at their destination. They must be massed in one direction to attain their object, just as the Sun's rays, when concentrated in a magnifying glass, ignite and create a fire. We must learn to control and direct our thoughts, and by persistent effort we will attain the goal; that is, a perfect concentration of thought at will, at any time, and in any direction desired.

The good news is that with the exercise of Concentration we can start to learn how to control what happens inside our body by training our thought power to willfully and consciously work inside our body. The following example can be a starting point: Everyday, let's find a time and a quiet place where we can retire for few minutes (our bedroom would be the most convenient).

Let's lay down and attempt to relax the muscles. The first sensation will be that of tensions in some parts of the body, which means that the blood circulation is being impeded by stress caused by our daily physical, mental, and emotional activities, or by illness. That part of the body is temporarily imprisoned and under siege by adversaries. Let's now attempt to remove such siege by first visualizing our body as a wonderful structure filled with vital energy. Now, let's imagine this vital energy or blood circulating inside the body. At a certain point, we can feel the vital energy being barred from accessing some parts of the system. Let's visualize that! We know that the vital fuel needs to flow without restrictions. Gently, but powerfully, let's imagine a thought-form of a concentrated energy under our control and let's deploy it in the area where we feel tensions and uneasiness. With the power of our will, let's command and direct distorted veins and cells to straighten them up and let the vital energy penetrate them. There is still resistance, and we can feel that part of the body decontracting and vibrating. Let's take a pause, recharge, and then repeat the shot again, and again, until all impediments have been removed. Finally, let's visualize the body filled with the vital energy flowing with no restriction. How do we feel after this exercise? We may try this and take notice of what would happen in our body, emotions, and mind. All it takes here is to try, because if we don't, we will not know firsthand how the force can move and model the matter!

We live in a world governed by the laws of nature. Under these laws we must live and work, and we are powerless to change them. If we know them and intelligently cooperate with them, these nature-forces become most valuable servants. If, on the other hand, we do not understand them and in our ignorance work contrary to them, they become most dangerous enemies, capable of terrible destruction. The goal of our evolution on earth is to emancipate us; to transform us from static creatures to dynamic creators. When we Emancipate ourselves from ignorance, we can Anticipate what work the Inner Power wants our personality to do, and when we know what needs to be done, we can Participate in all vital functions pertaining to our body and to the expansion of our consciousness.

To conclude, Concentration is the first step in our deliberate undertaking to connect our conscious mind with the Inner Power; our individual Inner God. By learning how to concentrate our thoughts, we train our mind to attract finer mental stuff and eliminate the unnecessary ones. We also sharpen them while they gain in both clarity and speed, so that confusion and agitation are progressively eliminated from the mind, giving us a poised and sane intellect, which will also contribute to a sound body and a soft heart.

When we have practiced Concentration for some time, focusing the mind upon some simple objects, creating a living Thought-Form by means of the imaginative faculty, we can, in the next step, by means of Meditation, learn all about the image thus created.

2. **Meditation**

From Latin *meditationem* (nominative *meditatio and the stem meditari*), to Meditate means to think over, to reflect, to consider, to ponder. The Latin verb also conveys the concepts of planning, devising, practicing, rehearsing, or studying. From a frequentative form of PIE root **medi,** which means *"Middle",* also the prefix of words *Medical, Medicine, Mediation, Media, Mediocracy,* but also found in words *intermediate, immediate,* to meditate implies to take appropriate measures, to discourse on a subject. The act of meditating is also construed to mean a continuous calm thought upon some subject.

Generally, when we talk about Meditation, we mean a practice during which we relax our mind to find peace and momentarily escape from the tumults of the daily business. As will be discussed in this section, some aspects of meditation can lead to such state of *interiorem pacem,* or inner peace. But, from its definition and etymology, meditation is far from a state of escapade, a relaxation, or a moment of peace. It is, in contrary, a state of intensely volitional mental activities committed to understanding, framing, studying, and solving problems. It is a moment of deep undertakings. In the same line, we sometimes confuse Meditation and Concentration, or we use the two terms interchangeably.

To clear this confusion, let's first remember that Concentration is a focus of the mind on one single thought, idea, or subject. Intense concentration builds a living thought form, a clear and true image. In meditation, on the other hand, we learn much about this thought form; that is, the exercise enables us to enter in the relationship between the thought, idea, or object to the world. In concentration we put all our attention on one subject or idea; in meditation we gather all knowledge possible upon this one subject. The mind ponders and gropes, always bringing added bits of information and, thereby, gaining new significance and new understanding. This process, when adhered to for some time, will enrich our own world of thought in such a way that we will be able to reach out into new fields of knowledge and gain new understanding there also. If we may talk in the language of photography, Concentration deals with the taking of the picture. We focus the camera on one object, press on the click, and grab the image. The goal is to capture the best image possible. Meditation, on the other hand, can be related to the understanding the processes that led to the wonderful picture we have, but also the analysis of such a picture.

To illustrate the above assertions, let's say we want to study the wooden table in our dining room. The first thing we do is to concentrate on it in order to build a thought form, a mind picture of our table as it stands in our dining room. During Concentration, we call up the image of a table and such thought form is clearly formed in the mind. Now, let's take the next step by following the processes involved in the making of the table. This is where the work of Meditation begins. Let's think of what kind of wood was needed for our table and where it came from. We go back to the time when, as a tiny seed, the tree from which the wood was cut first fell into the forest soil. We watch it grow from year to year, covered by the snows of winter and warmed by the summer Sun, steadily growing upward, its roots meanwhile constantly spreading under the ground. First it is a tender sapling, swaying in the breeze; then, as a young tree, it gradually stretches higher and higher toward the air and the sunshine. As the years pass, its girth becomes greater and greater, until at last one day the logger comes, with axe and saw gleaming as they reflect the rays of the winter's Sun. Our tree is felled and shorn of its branches, leaving but the trunk; that is cut into logs, which are hauled over the frozen roads to the river bank, there to await the springtime when the melting snow swells the streams. A great raft of the logs is made, the pieces of our tree being among them. We know every little peculiarity about them and would recognize them instantly among thousand, so clearly have we marked them in our mind.

We follow the raft down the stream, noting the passing landscape and become familiar with people who have the care of the raft and who sleep upon little camping huts built upon their floating charge. At last, we see it arriving at a sawmill and disbanded. One by one, the logs are grasped by prongs on an endless chain and hauled out of the water. Here comes one of our logs, the widest part of which will be made into the top of our table. It is hauled out of the water to the log deck and rolled about by workers with peeves. We hear the hungry whine of the great circular saws as they revolve so fast that they appear as mere blurs before our eyes. Our log is placed upon a carriage, which is propelled toward one of them, and in a moment those teeth of steel are tearing their way through its body and dividing it into boards and planks. Some of the wood is selected to form part of a building, but the best of it is taken to a furniture factory and put into a kiln where it is dried by steam so that it will not shrink after it has been made into furniture. Then, it is taken out and put through a great planning machine with many sharp knives, which makes it smooth.

Next, it is sawn off into different lengths and glued together to form table-tops. The legs are turned from thicker pieces and set into the frame that supports the top; then the whole article is smoothed again with sandpaper, varnished and polished, thus completing the table in every respect. It is next sent out, with other furniture, to the store where we bought it, and we follow it as it is carted from that place to our home and left in our dining room.

The above process can be applied to other subjects of our studies. If for example the subject of our concentration is a flower and we wish to meditate on it, after fixing our mind upon it steadily, we can visualize the seed as it is taken and buried in the ground. Presently, we shall see it burst, shooting forth its roots, which penetrate the Earth in a spiral manner. From the main branches of the roots we watch the myriads of minute rootlets, as they branch out and ramify in all directions. Then the stem begins to shoot upward, bursting through the surface of the Earth and coming forth as a tiny green stalk. It grows, now there is an off-set; a tiny twig shoots out from the main stem. It grows another offset and a branch appears; from the branches, little stalks with buds at the end shootout; presently there are a number of leaves. Then comes a bud at the top; it grows larger until it begins to burst and the red leaves of the rose show beneath the green. It unfolds in the air, emitting an exquisite perfume, which we sense perfectly as it is wafted to us on the balmy summer breeze that gently sways the beautiful creation before the mind's eye.

This is what meditation really is; a process of gathering, processing, and analyzing information on a given subject. Such exercise, when performed with consistent frequency, can help us learn more about things, ideas, or issues we are concerned with. The quality of information we collect will improve over time and will be proportional to the quality of our performance during the exercise. Thus, by meditation, we become conversant with the various branches of industry necessary to convert a forest tree into a piece of furniture, in the case of our table. We also make an acquaintance with mother nature and her marvelous ways of producing beautiful flowers. In the case of the table, we saw all the machines and the workers, and noted the peculiarities of the various places. In both cases of the table and the flower, we followed the life process whereby trees have grown from tiny seeds. We have also learned that back of seemingly very commonplace things there is a great and absorbingly interesting industry, history, and system. A computer, a cell phone, a car, a painting, a cable we use to bring electricity in our home, the electricity itself, or a business, a social organization, a political system, etc...., all have interesting histories well worth exploring.

But, like any analytical processes, Meditation comes with many components or sub-exercises that can be practiced separately while concurring to the same objective.

These components are Observation, Discrimination, Contemplation, and Adoration.

A- Observation

Observation is the use of the senses as means of obtaining information regarding phenomena around us. Observation and action generate the Conscious Soul. It is one of the most important aids we have in our efforts to realize the power of the Inner Power and gain direct conscious knowledge.

Most of us go through life blind-folded. It can be said, and it is literally true that we "have eyes, and see not; have ears, and hear not." With all the things that go in our world, our lack of observation adds to our deplorable conditions. The urban life has caused untold damage to our capacity to observe. We have friends, coworkers, and family members, but we can't describe the color of their eyes. We walk on a street for years, but we can't provide specific details of it. We live in a house and work in an office, but we can't tell how many windows the building has. We sometimes think of people who can provide thorough details of places, humans, and things as having special skills, or of being highly gifted. The truth is, these experts have spent years polishing their observation skills just as those who grow up in the countryside are used to it with great benefit. In the country, a child learns to use the muscles of the eyes and ears to the full extent, relaxing or contracting them as required to see and hear objects and sounds at considerable distances in the open or close at hand in and about the house. In urban life, in the opposite, we practically see *everything* close at hand and the muscles of our eyes are seldom used to observe objects at any great distance. That faculty is, therefore, to a large extent lost, resulting in a prevalence of nearsightedness and other viewing troubles. The same can be said of the hearing sense that is adversely impacted by the many confusing noises in the city. Some people however, are to some extent, excusable for this, because their sight and/or hearing are not normal. Some others are fully excusable, because their ears and eyes are completely impaired to see or to hear, but they can still gain a big deal of skills by observing through their other fully functioning senses such the smelling and touching. In any cases, for those who aspire to deep knowledge of things and to a life of full consciousness, it is very important that we practice observation and develop the ability to see, hear, feel all things about us in clear, definite outlines, and in full detail.

The value of accurate observation is of the highest importance to the development of the memory. The quality of our memory depends largely on the accuracy of the pictures we record from the outside surroundings. In this respect, there are two types of memories we build in our mind throughout life: a conscious or voluntary memory and unconscious or involuntary memory, also called subconscious. As indicated by the differences of terms conscious and unconscious, the processes of building these two memories are also different. In the first case, we, as thinking and individualized beings (Inner Power), function directly in the subtle realm of Abstract Thought, which we have specialized within the periphery of our individual aura. Through senses, we view, feel, touch, ear, or taste the impressions made by the outer world upon our sensory system, together with the feelings and emotions generated by them in the emotional system, and mirrored in the mind. From these mental images, using our cognitive system, we make conclusions concerning the subjects with which they deal. Those conclusions are ideas. With the will power, the Inner Power projects an idea through the mind where it takes concrete shape as a thought-form by drawing mind-stuff around itself from the realm of Concrete Thought.

Thus, when we volitionally observe something we wish to study, we consciously interact and record the picture of that thing in our conscious memory. Later, we can close our senses and recall at will that very picture to our mind with the same clarity, details, and with as much life as the material thing itself.

This is the same process we use when we try to take a picture of something. Using the same example of taking a picture we used previously in the section on Concentration, let's imagine that we have the best camera and walk in a given location to take pictures. After selecting a target, we point our camera to it and we adjust the lenses to get the best image possible. When we have the perfect angle, we point the lenses to the target and press the trigger, and voila! We have the beautiful image recorded on the memory of the camera. With today's digital tools, we can manipulate the same image to give it as many new features as we wish. What we have recorded here is the conscious memory of our photographic adventure. We consciously and voluntarily record what we wish to record.

Involuntary memory, on the other hand, comes to us in a different way than voluntary memory, and altogether beyond our control. Building on the above example, let's say that we are taking a picture in the local park. This time, while our focus is on the target, we cannot stop the camera from recording many other things surrounding the target. Our main selected picture is not the end of the story, for even as we captured the most precise picture, the camera will more likely and inevitably capture many other details we did not intend to record. That is, a child playing with parents in the background, a falling leaf, a sudden change in the sky, a spectacular rainbow, etc...may end up recorded on the memory of our camera as so that without our expressed intent, the ether will carry to the sensitive film in the camera an accurate impression of the surrounding landscape, taking in the minutest detail regardless of whether we have observed it or not. Those unintended recordings become our involuntary memory, some of which can be easily detected, while some others can go undetected for long periods of time, or even forever.

The same happens to us during our interactions with the outside world; the ether contained in the air we inspire carries with it an accurate and detailed picture of all our surroundings, not only of material things, but also the conditions existing each moment within our aura. The slightest thought, feeling, or emotion is transmitted to the lungs, where it is injected into the blood, recording the memory of all things that were captured by both our voluntary and involuntary interactions with the world. These pictures may escape the reach of our conscious mind, but not that of the Inner Power who sees, feels, knows all things. Similarly, and as discussed earlier, though our conscious mind is unaware of what is going on inside our body during the normal functionality, the Inner Power is nevertheless in close touch with the whole system in which it can experience discomfort when the system malfunctions. By properly exercising concentration, meditation, or prayer, the Inner Power can release part or all our involuntary memory and make it available to our conscious mind as described in the first chapter. The same exercises are powerful tools that can help our conscious mind progressively gain control of vital functions happening inside our bodies.

To come back to the value of accurate observation, if the record of the voluntary memory matches that from involuntary observations, we can expect increase in our mental strength, great feelings, and body harmony. We all recall the joy and the comfort we sometimes feel when we can remember details of some forgotten scenes. On the hand, if the two memories are conflicted, the rhythm and harmony of our body is disturbed in the proportion of the inaccuracy of our voluntary observation. We can likewise recall the pain and uneasiness we experience when we have trouble remembering some important details of things. Frustration, confusion, and even pain often follow unsuccessful effort to connect dots on things we may have had a clear memory of in the past. Good sleep may partially restore body harmony, but the warring discordances from day to day and year to year are one of the causes that gradually harden and destroy our body until it becomes unfit for the use of the Inner God and must be abandoned. In proportion, and as will be discussed later, when we learn how to observe accurately and to build an accurate memory, we shall gain in health and longevity, and we shall need less rest and sleep.

B- Critical Thinking

When we have learned to systematically observe our surrounding, drawing conclusions from observed scenes and actions, the next meditative practice consists of learning how to discriminate; that is, to think critically, to cultivate the faculty of logical reasoning, logic being the best teacher in the physical world, as well as the safest and surest guide in any field of study.

While practicing discrimination, we should always keep in mind that critical thinking is all about gathering facts and not for criticism, at least not wanton criticism. Constructive criticism, which points out defects and the means of remedying them, is the basis of progress; but destructive criticism, which vandalistically demolishes good and bad alike without aiming at any higher attainment, is an ulcer on the character and must be eradicated. Gossip, conspiracy theories, and idle tale-bearing are clogs and hindrances. While it is not required that we shall say that black is white and overlook manifestly wrong conduct, criticism should be made to help advance ideas or discussions, not to wantonly besmirch the character of a fellow being only because we have found a little stain. Remembering the parable of the mote and the beam, we should turn our most unsparing criticism toward ourselves, to our own ideas, thoughts, and actions. We will learn the value of self-criticism and self-evaluation in the later section. For now, let's say that no one is so perfect that there is no room for improvement. The more blameless we deem ourselves, the less prone we are to find fault and cast the first stone at others. Remembering the Power of the word, if we point out faults and suggest ways for improvement, it must be done without personal feeling and in an amical tone of voice. We must always seek the good that is hidden in everything.

The cultivation of this attitude in Discrimination is particularly important, especially in this era of rapid and explosive flow of information, information manipulation, and polarization. Many of us easily align with whatever idea or slogans that gratifies our sense of right and makes us feel good. But, by learning the skill of discrimination and critical thinking, we maximize our chances of reaching correct conclusions and gather first-hand knowledge, while eliminating opportunities of wasting the valuable Thought Power we have worked so hard to develop by rejecting logic and ponderance. Discrimination is therefore the faculty whereby we distinguish what is important and essential, from what is not; separating the real from illusion, and the lasting from the evanescent. For example, we are accustomed to think of our physical body as true and whole self. From this way of thinking comes both the cult of body and physical traits, and the shaming of it. But Discrimination teaches us that every human being is a living invisible Force and our bodies are but temporary dwelling places, instruments the Inner Power uses to learn, expand, and bring about changes in our universe. Just as a carpenter uses hammer and saw as important instruments but does not think of him/herself as being either, neither should we identify ourselves with our bodies, races, nations, etc...., but learn to discriminate, to regard the form as a servant, valuable only in so far as it serves the purpose of the Inner God. This is probably what Christ meant when he declared that "before Abraham was, I AM" ([11]) and therefore expressing the truth that the I AM or the Inner Power existed before all races, genders, nations, etc.... When we understand who we really are in such a perspective, we shall find that the Inner Power can take us to levels of development impossible to image otherwise. Finally, just as the practice of Observation contributes to the building of a Conscious Soul, Discrimination contributes to the development of an Intellectual Soul and gives us our first start toward the conscious connection with our Inner God.

When we have practiced Observation and Discrimination for some time, and have become fairly

---

[11] John 8:48-59

familiar with them, there are still higher stages in the Meditation that can be taken. These stages are Contemplation and Adoration, which many people refer to when they speak of meditation as a peaceful moment of relaxation and escapade.

C- Contemplation and Adoration

As mentioned previously, Concentration is concerned with focusing thought upon a single object. It is the means whereby we build a clear, objective, and living image of the thing, idea, or subject about which we wish to acquire knowledge. In Meditation - with Observation and Discrimination components - we trace the developmental path of the thing, idea, or subject we have been concentrating on. We explore, analyze, and dissect it to pick out every shred of evidence and details as to its relation to the world in general. These two mental exercises deal, in the deepest and most thorough manner imaginable, with *things (forms)*. Contemplation and Adoration, on the other hand, go behind forms to deal with the forces, the very *soul of things*.

First, during Contemplation there is no reaching out in thought or imagination for the sake of getting information as was the case in Observation and

Discrimination. It is simply the holding of the object before our mental vision and letting the soul of it speak to us. We sit quietly and relax upon a couch or bed, not negatively, but thoroughly on the alert, watching for the information that will surely come if we have reached the proper development. Then, the *Form* of the object seems to vanish, and we see only the *Life* at work. Contemplation will teach us about the Life side, as other segments of Meditation taught us about the Form side.

When we reach this stage and have before us for example, the image of the tree in the forest - the same tree that gave us the table to concentrate on and which we followed the journey during Meditation - this time we lose sight of the form entirely to see only the Life, which in this case is the life of a group of plants to which our tree belongs; a group spirit. We may find, to our astonishment, that the group spirit of the tree includes the various insects that feed upon it; that the parasite and its host are emanations from one and the same group spirit, for the higher we ascend in the invisible realms, the fewer the separate and distinct forms, and the more completely the One Life predominates, impressing upon us the supreme fact that there is but only One Life, only One Force in the universe; the Universal Life of God, the Great Arche-Tekton, in Whom we live, and move, and have our being. Minerals, plants, animals, and humans; all, without exception, are manifestations of this one Life, for God is Life.

Having reached this height by Contemplation and having realized that we are in truth beholding God in the Life that permeates all things, there remains still to be taken the highest step; Adoration, whereby we unite ourselves with the Source of all things. Reaching the Source sounds impossible and we think of it in terms of apocalyptic fiction; of Neo arriving to the heart of the Matrix after defeating all enemies and losing his loved ones. Though we may not get to this level, what's more important is that we start the journey. Sometimes, the journey is more important than the destination. What is necessary is that we start to improve ourselves and to earnestly and *persistently* continue therein to sharpen our mind, emotions, and Thought Power. The time required to bring results from the performance of the exercises varies with each individual and is dependent upon each person's application. Therefore, no general time can be set. Some, who are almost ready may obtain results in a few days or weeks;

others have to work months, years, and even their whole life without *visible* results, yet the results will be there and the pilgrim who faithfully persists will someday behold his/her patience and faithfulness rewarded, in this life or the next, and the inner World will open its gaze, finding him/herself a citizen of realms where the opportunities are immeasurably greater than what our mind can grasp.

But, let us clearly imprint this in our mind: no matter how eager we may be to undertake our Daily Quest, we should never neglect our professional and other social duties. There is a good reason why we must live in the din of a busy world for the sake of needed experiences. These experiences are actually the most important indicators of *clues* we need to assess our readiness for, performance of, and level in the Quest. Our daily duties are the rough material we need for the Daily Quest. At the same time, no matter the circumstance of our daily duties, we can and should take moments of silence for concentration and meditation. These exercises are a great deal of gears we have in gaining soul growth and we can use them to build an invisible Living Sanctuary (*Sancti Spiritus*) where we can enter whenever we need to restore our physical, mental, and emotional harmony so dear to our development, but also to pray God in spirit and in truth.

3. **Prayer**

The word Prayer comes from the PIE root *"prek"* and modern Latin *precari*. To pray means "to ask earnestly, to request, to beg, to entreat". Taken this way, Prayer implies an effort to reach out or to network, to share, interact, and exchange with others. It also sets out the idea of relationship and conversation between one individual with another, or, as used in religion, a relationship between a person and God.

Much has been written about Prayer, for it is universal. From the primitive to modern times, all people have been addressing a Great Spirit, a Supreme Being, either with fear and trembling, or with adoration and confidence. The divine origin of everyone makes itself felt and the divine Spark in us yearns to recognize the high Source of all beings.

Every day's life teaches us that when we encounter life challenges and sorrows, or when we achieve success, we reach out to friends, family, coworkers, communities, or to public and private institutions to either ask for help, support, comfort, or to provide the same to those in need. We also enjoy the company of others to either compete for success or fun; to express gratitude for good deeds received and receive the same for our good deeds; to praise or to congratulate others and be congratulated by them in return; to ask for forgiveness for our wrongdoings or to forgive others for their trespasses. When we take such actions, we engage in an act of prayer by either making a plea, a request to other people or entities, or by allowing others to make similar request to us. Life is incontestably a constant act of Prayer and a rendez-vous of giving and receiving! Above all interactions we have with our world, our personality yearns for a special relationship with a higher power that can support us, help us, and sustain us when all other sources of support and comfort falter.

Most of us turn to God as presented to us by the religion we practice, by the culture we grew up with, or the one we have adopted. But, in some instances, rather than calling for an outside God, something compels us to introvert our thought and feeling to find a source of comfort and support from within ourselves. By doing so, we acknowledge the existence of the Inner Power, we establish a channel of direct communication with our individual Inner God, Whom, as already explained, is one with the God of the universe. Thus, when we pray, we turn our thoughts to God, we engage God in a conversation, we thank and praise God, and ask for help for many of our concerns.

We approach God in confession, supplication, and adoration, but also often feel the need to ask for material sustenance. Whether directed to the outside God or to God Within, Prayer is like the turning on of an electric switch. It does not create electricity, but it simply provides a channel through which the electric power may flow. In like manner, Prayer creates a channel through which the Power of our Inner God may pour itself into our conscious mind and personality. If the switch were made of wood or glass, it would be of no use; in fact, it would be a barrier that the electric energy could not possibly pass, because that is contrary to its nature. To be effective, the switch must be made of a conducting metal, for then it is in harmony with the laws of electrical manifestation. Similarly, and as discussed below, Prayer must be supported by faith and made of genuine thoughts and intentions, not just a mumbling of saucy words and fanatically pathetic gestures designed to please some like-minded audiences.

The general idea is that when we pray to God, we must always ask for something that happens to be often of material nature and for self-benefit. This idea takes the view that as God is our provider of all things, we may go to our heavenly father/mother in prayer and s/he is bound to give us whatever that we desire. If we do not get it the first time, we need only keep praying, and because of our very importunity, our wish will be granted. Such a view is repellent not only in terms of spiritual enlightened, but if we bring the matter down to a practical basis, it is evident that a wise father/mother having a son/daughter able to provide for him/herself would naturally resent it if this son/daughter should appear before the parent several times a day with importunate requests for this, that, and the other thing, which he/she could easily obtain by going to work and earning.

Let us mark this in golden letters in our mind and heart: **Prayer, no matter how earnest and sincere, can never replace work**. If we work for a good purpose with our whole heart, soul, and body, and at the same time pray God to bless our work, there is no doubt that the petition will be granted every time. In other words, unless we put our shoulder to the wheel, we have no right to call on the Deity for assistance. As the example of the electric switch shows, the main object of prayer is to get us into as close communication with God as possible, in order that the Divine Life and Light may flow into us, enlighten us, and enable us to realize our divine nature and contribute to the creative work. When we pray God to bless our work, our hands, mind, and heart instead, we endeavor for spiritual illumination; we ask for things we cannot procure ourselves by any available means, and for things that can benefit to others and contribute to the progress of humankind. Instead of asking for light, let's ask for eyes to see it; instead of sweeter songs, let's ask for ears to hear them; instead of power, let's ask for the wisdom to use it; instead of love, let's ask for the skill to turn a frown into a caress; instead of short living joys, let's ask for the ability to feel the kindling presence of the inner God and to give to others all we have of courage and cheer; instead of material gifts, let's ask for the sense of better use the one we already possess, such as the power to dominate all fears, to think critically, to be the friend we wish to be, to speak the truth, to seek the good, and to encourage all humans to live in harmony, in a total respect of their freedom to choose. When we pray in this manner, we stand in the receptive state that brings us nearer to our ideal where we may experience an outpouring of the Inner Power, radiant and glorious. Then, we will have learned by first-hand experience that prayer is a powerful method used in perfecting our ability to recognize, interact with, and express the presence of the Inner Power.

This brings to mind another important point: the place of Prayer and the vibrations that are inside and outside it. Every prayer, spoken or unspoken, every song of praise, and every reading of parts of the scriptures which teach or exhort, if done by a properly prepared reader who loves and lives what s/he reads, can bring down upon both the worshipers and place of worship an outpouring of spiritual power. This in time will build an invisible church, temple, or mosque around the physical structure, which in the case of a devout congregation becomes so beautiful that it transcends all imagination and defies description. This invisible edifice is A LIVING THING, vibrant with divine power of immense aid to worshipers, for it helps them in adjusting the tangled vibrations of the world which permeate their auras when they enter a true "House of God" to get into the proper attitude of prayer. Then, during prayer, it helps them to lift themselves in aspiration to the throne of divine grace and to offer there their praise and adoration which call forth from the Higher Power a new outpouring of the spirit in the loving response. But such places are scarce, for a REAL sanctuary is required in scientific prayer. No gossip or profane conversation may take place in or near it for that spoils the vibrations; voices must be hushed and the attitude reverent; each must bear in mind that s/he stands upon holy ground and act accordingly. Furthermore, the power of prayer increases enormously with each additional worshiper.

Sometimes, we wonder whether we should pray alone or in a group. First, based on the principle that one coal cannot make the fire, but when several coals are put together, the heat within each can be kindled into a flame emitting light and warmth, when we unite our prayers with others who are of like mind, much can be accomplished. Collective prayer in places of worship is helpful when done in an atmosphere of reverence and quietude as mentioned before. The increase in efficacy may be compared to geometrical progression if the worshipers are properly attuned and trained in COLLECTIVE prayer; the very opposite may result if they are not. Perhaps an illustration may make the principle clear. Let's suppose a group of musicians who have never played with others and who perhaps are not very proficient in the use of their instruments, were brought together and set to play in concert. It needs no keener imagination to realize that their first attempts would be marked by much discord, and were an amateur allowed to play with them, or even with a finished orchestra, no matter how earnest and how intense his/her desire, s/he would inevitably spoil their music. Similar scientific conditions govern collective prayer; to be efficacious participants must be equally well prepared to be in harmony with one another. However, unless we can have the harmony and peaceful cooperation in sacred places, it is better that we enter our own sanctuary and pray in secret. God knows our hidden thoughts and the sincerity of our motives. The Inner God is our true self in the highest expression. There is no thought, feeling, action, or inaction that can escape the gaze of this force whether we are alone or in a group. Thus, praying to the Inner Power, alone or in public, is the same as praying to God.

Building on the above assertion, no matter how we pray, collectively or in private, with words or in silence, the keyword is "repetition." By earnest, repeated prayer we not only acquire the habit of daily communion with our Inner Power, but this communion will also lift us up on wings of power and aspiration. It is, however, as will be seen, essential that we put intense earnestness into our devotional exercise. Otherwise, our monotonous repetition becomes mere habit, and we are in danger of saying empty words. When we dedicate ourselves wholeheartedly to the highest level, then prayer becomes the most powerful method of soul growth. But such dedication must be supported by strong pillars without which prayer cannot be sustainable.

The Nine Pillars of Prayer

Before expanding on the these nine pillars, it is important to point out that whether we pray for general good such as peace, healing, for thanksgiving, or for personal illumination, we should always keep in mind that it is a privilege to be in the presence of the Higher Power and to offer ourselves as channels to receive and liberate the force of peace, healing, or thanksgiving. This force comes from God, but before it can be transmitted, it must have been generated in our mind and heart; and to do this efficiently, we should understand accurately the mechanism of prayer and how it works. It is not enough that we know in a vague way of the sickness, wars, suffering that are in the world, and that we have a dim and hazy idea of how to help alleviate this suffering, whether it be bodily, emotional, or mental. To obtain the result for what we pray for, we must meet definite conditions. These conditions are the nine important values we all cherish in life as factors of success and happiness, but which when harnessed and embedded in our daily experiences, make our prayer efficacious, enjoyable, and effective.

I - Intensity of Concentration

The first value or pillar is the intensity of concentration. For our prayer to be effective, it must be accompanied by a good dose of Intensity in thought and feelings. Prayer is sometimes confused with Concentration and Meditation. But, as previously discussed, the exercise of concentration is all about focusing thought upon a single point as the Sun's rays are focused by means of a magnifying glass. We have learned earlier that Concentration is the direct application of thought power to the mental image of a certain definite object that may be good or evil according to the character of the person who practices it and the purpose for which s/he desires to use it. In this aspect, Prayer is similar to concentration.

Both Concentration and Prayer are powerful energies, the nature and objective, but also the use of which depend on the character of the person who generates the power. But, while the efficacy of prayer, as discussed below, depends largely upon the intensity of concentration, the devotional attitude and emotional outburst we express during prayer renders the latter far more efficacious than cold concentration can ever be. In this, Prayer differs from Concentration. As a matter of fact, it is exceedingly difficult for many of us to concentrate our thoughts coolly, calmly, and exclude all other considerations from our consciousness without the slightest emotion. In the case of prayer, the devotional attitude is more easily cultivated, for the mind is then centered on Deity. Thus, when we add emotions or devotion to concentration, our prayer becomes something more than the normal intellectual concentration. But what gives Prayer a turbo boost is the intensity of concentration.

To illustrate why such intensity is necessary in prayer, let's take the water spout as an example. We may not have seen this phenomenon of nature, but it is wonderful and awe inspiring. Usually, at the time it occurs, the sky seems to hang very low over the water; there is a tense feeling of depression or concentration in the air. Gradually, it seems as if a point in the sky reaches down toward the water, and the waves in a certain spot seem to leap upward until both sky and water meet in a swirling mass.

Something similar takes place when a person or several persons are in earnest prayer. When a person is intensely in earnest supplication to a Higher Power, his/her aura seems to form itself into a funnel shaped figure resembling the lower part of the water spout. This leaps up into space a great distance and, being attuned to the cosmic vibration of the universal life, it draws thence a divine power that enters the person or a group of persons, and ensouls the thought form they have created. Thus, the object for which they have united will be accomplished. But, as already stressed, let this be borne thoroughly in mind that the process of praying or concentrating is not a cold intellectual process. There must be a good amount of feeling adequate to accomplish the desired object, and unless this intensity of feeling is present, the object will not be realized. This is the secret of all the miraculous prayers that have been recorded; the person who prayed for something was always intensely in earnest; his/her whole being went into the desire for the thing for which s/he prayed, and thus lifted him/herself up into the very realms of the divine and brought down the response from God.

II - Work

Words and thoughts of prayer alone, so intense they may b e, will not bring about the desired result. Unless our whole life, waking and sleeping, is a living act of prayer for illumination and sanctification, our prayers will never penetrate to the Divine Presence and bring down upon us a flow of force from the Inner Power. "ORA ET LABORA" - pray and work - is an injunction we all must obey, or we will be met with but scant success. As pointed out previously, we can't just say words and prayer of peace, health, and gratitude, and engage in completely opposite thoughts and behavior, but expect our wish to manifest *deus ex machina*. We must accompany our thoughts and prayer with corresponding work for what we pray for. There is no better way to praise God than by good deeds!

There is an ancient anecdote about St. Francis of Assisi that can shed light upon the nature of a sustainable Work-Prayer dedicated to the service of God. One day, St. Francis stepped up to a young brother in the monastery with the invitation: "Come, brother, let us go down to the village and preach to the people." The young brother responded with alacrity, overjoyed at the prospect of a walk with the holy father, for he knew what a source of spiritual upliftment it would be. And so, they walked to the village, up and down its various streets and lanes, all the while conversing upon topics of absorbing spiritual interest, and finally turned their steps homeward towards the monastery. Then, suddenly it dawned upon the young brother that they had been so absorbed in their own conversation that they had forgotten the object of their walk to the village. Diffidently, he reminded St. Francis of the omission, and the latter responded: "Son, while we were walking the village streets the people were watching us, they overheard snatches of conversation and noted that we were talking of the love of God and His dear Son, our Savior; they noted our kindly greetings and our words of cheer and comfort to the afflicted ones we met, and even our garb spoke to them the language and call of religion; so we have preached to them every moment of our sojourn among them to must better purpose than if we had harangued them for hours in the marketplace." St. Francis had no other thought but God and to do good in His name. Therefore, he was well attuned to the divine vibration, and it is no wonder than when he went to his regular prayers, he was a powerful magnet for the divine Life and Light that permeated his whole being.

As busy people engaged in the secular work of the world and sometimes forced to do things that seem sordid, we often feel that we are hampered and hindered on such account. But if we "do all things as unto the God" and are "faithful over a few things," we shall find that in time opportunities will come of which we do not dream. As the magnetic needle temporarily deflected from the North by outside pressure instantly and eagerly returns to its natural position when the pressure is removed, so we must cultivate that yearning for our Inner God who will instantly turn our thoughts to the divine when our work in the world is done for the day and we are free to follow our own bent. We must cultivate a feeling similar to that which ensouls young lovers when, after an absence, they fly into each other's arms in an ecstasy of delight. This is an absolutely essential preparation for prayer, and if we fly to our God in that manner, the divine presence and voice will teach and cheer us beyond our fondest hopes.

III - The Universal Bank

Many of us are used to think that we should be able to get everything we want simply by praying to God or by making some forms of affirmation. That would be the same as to hoping to withdraw cash from a bank without first making the necessary deposits. It is the equivalence of trying to "get something for nothing", or to build a house with no materials, etc. If such thinking is considered awkward in our human relationships, we should strive to avoid it in our relationship with God, whom we can't cheat on.

In fact, there is an invisible institution we may call the "Universal Bank". Whether or not we realize it, whether we acknowledge it or not, we constantly and continually make deposits into this all-important institution. Every good thought, good feeling, and good action makes a deposit in our personal account. All our constructive work, our self-discipline, our service to others, and all our other actions that are in harmony with the cosmic order of things are deposits we make in our Universal Bank. These deposits are the source from which we draw our destiny, our good fortune, and our opportunities. The unseen Director of this Bank and agents keeps an unerring record of all deposits. From time to time, the Director declares a dividend in the form of some opportunity, success, good luck, or windfall.

Although nothing can ever happen by chance, most of us think that these things happen more or less accidentally. We are mistaken! The Inner Power within each of us is a high official of that Bank and has much to do with the declaration of dividends. Since the Universal Bank is backed by the Universe, it cannot fail. We can neither lose nor be defrauded of anything that is really ours. What is ours will come to us. There is never a mistake in the cosmic credit in which this bank deals. If our destiny and success are not what we would like them to be, then it is because our credit in the Universal Bank has been temporarily depleted. We should not waste to much of our time and energy to blame others, God, and the universe for our misfortunes. Neither should we indulge in envying other people we think have good fortune to their side. In such a case, the only thing that can get us out of indigent situation is to get busy and make new deposits in our Universal Account.

As stated above, we make deposits to our credit by constructive work, service, and self-discipline. We may be sure that our diligence in these respects will soon greatly improve opportunities and circumstances. If praying can also be compared to the banking operations, it can be said that when we pray, we are making new deposits and savings to neutralize and offset some of the debts of our previous transactions. Thus, we see that our destiny is all *self-created;* luck and chance are only apparent and are in truth created by us in the past. The most difficult, but also the most uplifting lesson we must learn in this respect is that we are surrounded with the materialization of our past thoughts, feelings, and acts. The overcoming of undesirable traits and the building up and reformation of character are most potent means of making deposits in the Universal Bank.

Finally, the Universal Bank is the storage for the Universal Supply. In our prayer, we may at any time demand the materialization of any specific thing, but we should leave that to the Inner God who knows the size of our deposit in the Universal Bank and who has the wisdom to do it properly. If we demand and specify certain materialization of our thought creations, we are very likely to make a mess of it and get something we don't need. "Think of What You Ask for!".

IV - The law of Giving and Receiving

One reason why we don't achieve success in our prayer is that we unconsciously or ignorantly violate the Law of Giving and Receiving. There really is a cosmic law administered by unseen forces that decrees that in order to receive, one must first give. This law is connected to the

Universal Bank. By sharing what we have, we open the channel that permits an inflow of the desirable things into our lives. The saying: "Give, and it shall be given unto you, good measure, pressed down, and shaken together, and running over...for with the same measure that you measure with, it shall be measured to you again" is universal truth. An understanding and acceptance of this law, and an intelligent effort to comply with it, eventually will bring a change for the better in our affairs.

V - The Golden Rule

The Golden Rule is another pillar for a successful and powerful prayer. "Do unto others as you would have others do unto you". This rule is unequivocal. It definitely tells us to do good to others at all times, under all conditions, regardless of what they do to us. The rule is impersonal; the conduct of the other person does not enter into the case. If disregarded, unpleasant effects are sure to follow. Putting it into practice eventually will bring a decided improvement in our environment and material conditions. It gives a magnetic personality; one that attracts others and enlists their help and cooperation in carrying out projects. It creates a magnetic force that is a means of increasing success in all lines. We should never allow resentment, caused by mistreatment from others, to prevent us from doing to them as we would like them to do to us. It really pays to carry out the Golden Rule, which is not merely a religious ideal.

VI - Forgiveness

Forgiveness is a powerful tool we cannot afford to neglect. Forgiveness is scientific and spiritual. It brings into play the forces of the unseen planes about us. It dissolves the thought forms of hate, revenge, and ill-will, and prevents their materialization into adverse fortune. Unforgiveness, which includes resentment, grudges, and revenge, often materializes into some of the unhappiest conditions of life, particularly if allowed to continue by habitual thinking along those lines. Hatred is the most destructive force in the Universe. Hatred is a dangerous poison against physical, mental, emotional health. Unforgiveness and revenge are phases of hate. Revenge is the deadliest of passions; it surely will frustrate success. In fact, it is literally impossible to relate to the Inner Power when our heart is cramped by unforgiveness and our thought darkened by hatred. No matter what happens to us in the course of our daily life, we cannot afford to hold resentment or to indulge in revengeful thoughts. We can be perfectly sure if someone has mistreated us that the law of the land and unseen laws of God will bring them whatever retribution they merited.

It is also vital that we seek to find good in everything and every situation, no matter how lacking it may seem on the surface. The mere act of looking for good makes a thought form that will in time materialize into more good, more success, more favorable conditions. Looking for good is like starting a snowball that grows in size as it rolls downhill. That also is a property of all thought forms. Those of alike nature combine and grow rapidly. This equally applies to looking for the good. The good in our environment very definitely can be increased by the practice of this principle. Praise is an extension of this. Praise is like sunlight - the sunlight of the soul. It promotes both goodwill and success. We must praise what is good in others wherever there is the slightest excuse for doing so. And above all, we must not forget to praise and thank the Inner Power each day for the life, the guidance, and the supply of all our needs. Again, all things come from this Power.

VII - Faith

As for Faith, let's say that because Prayer, as

previously mentioned, is like an electrical switch that opens a channel along which electricity may flow from the power-grid into our house, Faith is like the energy which turns the switch. Without muscular force we cannot turn the switch to obtain physical light, and without faith we cannot pray in such a manner as to secure spiritual illumination. Faith is the force in us we can deploy to open the channel of communication with the Inner God. Doubt, on the other hand, has a most withering and blighting influence on our life. That such are the effects of faith and doubt can easily be seen by examining their influence in our daily life. We know how expressions of faith and trust buoy us up and how depressing is the effect on us when we are doubted by others.

Many of us are used to think of Faith as a religious directive. Faith is rather natural and scientific, although religion claims the monopoly of it. As a matter of fact, whether we know it or not, we live by faith every minute of our lives, and in proportion that we so live, are we happy or miserable. For example, at night we lie down to sleep secure in the *faith* that no harm will disturb our slumbers, that we shall wake in the morning and be able to go through our appointed tasks the next day. Were it not for that faith; were doubts on the above points to assail, would we dare to lay our heads upon our pillows? Could we close our eyes in calm slumber? Surely not; and in a short time we should be physical and mental wrecks, hastened into a premature grave by the demon of doubt. When we go to the store to buy groceries, or when we order food from a restaurant, we have *faith* in the rectitude of the merchants; we are satisfied that they will give us wholesome viands and not poisoned good. If not, how miserable our lives would be? instead of enjoying our food, doubt would take away our appetite so that we should be unable to eat a wholesome meal, for even food would be poisoned by our mental state of doubt and fear.

Furthermore, some of us have watched the shadow of the Earth when projected upon the Moon at an eclipse of the Moon and realized that the round shadow is the only positive proof of the rotundity of the Earth. Yet, we all say as a matter of truth that the Earth is round. We know this, not first hand, but only by *faith* in other people's statements. So, with the fact that we are traveling through space at the rate of one thousand miles an hour by virtue of the Earth's motion on its own axis, and the still more astonishing scientific fact that, while the Earth appears to be so still and motionless, it is in reality traveling in its orbit around the sun at the rate of 1,600,000 miles in twenty-four hours. These and many other similar facts that we cannot possibly investigate for ourselves we accept and live by every day of our lives; we call them knowledge and we stake our lives and our happiness upon them by virtue of *faith*. Finally, by faith we leave our homes in the morning *trusting* to the law of gravity to keep them in the same place till we return at night. Thus, we see that doubt and skepticism have a withering and blighting effect upon the object directed against, while faith opens and expands our mental capacity as sunlight unfolds the beautiful flower. Therefore, and as stated in the first chapter, we understand the necessity for faith when approaching the Inner Power.

Let it be clearly understood that faith we are talking about here is not a blind faith, not an unreasoning faith that clings to a creed or dogma contrary to reason, but an open and unbiased state of the mind that is ready to weigh any proposition until thorough investigation has proven it untenable. Moreover, the required Faith is a translation of belief and action. The Church always emphasizes the necessity of faith, while the Science emphasizes and places its reliance on Work. But, when faith flowers into work we can reach the highest ideal of expression.

VIII - Thought Control

As discussed earlier, our Thought is the most powerful tool we have to help us gain knowledge and transform the world. It is also a link that connects our conscious mind to the Inner Power. When writing to his Roman fellows, the apostle Paul urged them *"not to be conformed to common way of thinking, but be transformed by the renewal of mind, that by testing they may discern what is the will of God, what is good and acceptable, and perfect"* ([12]). In the same line, we must emphasize that wrong thinking blocks us from realizing the power of the Inner God, that happiness resides solely in the mind, and that by thought control and thought substitution we have the key to happiness and success.

When we change our thoughts from negative to positive, pessimistic to optimistic, selfish to loving, doubtful to faithful, we make ourselves receptive to and let the Inner Power release its energy and work miracles in our lives. Health will be restored, mental conditions will be changed, and we can use our imagination to make mental

---

[12] Romans 12:2

pictures of improved health and these pictures will blend with other thought forms of strength and courage and become a part of the instrument of release. We will find that we are no longer the slave of ill health, bad luck, or continuous failure. We will find that health is the normal accompaniment of poise and of a balanced emotional condition. With health will come a greater ability for success in work and in all material lines. When we *reform* our Thought, we undertake an effort to *conform* to the directives from the Inner Power, which is return gives us renewed strength, courage, and confidence to *perform* well when new opportunities come to us.

Happiness resides solely in the mind. External conditions have an influence on happiness only as we allowed them to affect the making of thought forms through the mind. Thought forms have the property of clothing themselves with that substance of the invisible plane which we know as emotion. If we think thoughts of optimism and happiness, emotional substance of happiness is built into the mind, and we are happy regardless of all material and bodily conditions. If, on the other hand, we make thought forms of fear and failure, they build into the mind the emotional substance of unhappiness, and we would be unhappy even if we had all the wealth of the world and even if our health were perfect. For example, let's suppose that someone very close to us were undergoing a surgical operation. Naturally, we would feel very much concerned and our feelings would probably swing between fear and hope. Sometimes one emotion and sometimes the other would predominate. But, let's consider what would be the effect upon the patient if we were to voice our doubt and misgivings on every occasion. Fear always has a devitalizing and detrimental effect that makes it very difficult for a patient to recover, particularly as during the time of an illness s/he is less self-assertive and more negative than at times when s/he is in good, robust health. While we, with reason, may really be anxious to help him/her and would do anything in our power to save him/her, by that attitude of mind and the expression of such thoughts, we could also be really hindering him/her very much.

In conclusion, there are three little formulas for self-help that can help control our thought:

First, Positive Thought. This means keeping the mind habitually positive and alert, not relaxed and inert. Positive thought automatically shuts out a crowd of tramp thoughts and desires that are floating through the mental atmosphere. When these thoughts are shut out, they cease to be an influence in life, and our mental creations become far better with a decided increase in the materialization of the desirable things of life.

Second, the Golden Key: when in trouble, when fearful of losing money, friends, or job, when something of value is lost, we should not continue to make thought forms of these undesired losses, which would add to the general depression. We should, instead, reverse the process and *think of God, while taking appropriate concrete steps to address the problem.* There is a time for expressing shock, for grieving, but also for recovery. However, even as we are under shock and grief, we cannot afford to shut the door to the Inner Power, because God from Within includes all desirable things. By refusing to over think our misfortune and by constantly thinking of the Inner God, we are making thought forms of strength, beauty, goodness, and success, even though unconsciously. These, in due time, will materialize into good and the calamity feared will have been averted.

Third, the Power of Duty: duty performed one day at a time has the power to create enough good to get us through the day; tomorrow will be another day in which the process can be repeated. Duties performed with love are a way of liberation. This is a vital key to success over any period of life. The success that comes as a result of duty performed will not always be the kind that we would have selected, but it will be true success from the standpoint of the Inner God, and that is the main thing. Moreover, in due time, this will resolve itself into a form of success that will be easily recognized and admitted as the best kind. In the meantime, we will be relieved of fear and anxiety because we know that everything will come out alright in the end. Thus, through the power of duty performed, we will become able to *live by faith* in the Inner Power, which is the most fundamental secret of success in life, including work, health, and the supply of all material needs.

IX - Confession

We may have heard much concerning confession. Perhaps we thought it of no value. We may have thought that confessing our wrongdoings to a priest or a minister would have no effect. Nevertheless, there is a very important metaphysical principle concealed in it; namely, *confession dissipates the emotional force built into thought forms of past wrongdoing, releases it, and helps to restore poise to the personality.* When wrong is done that involves fear, shame, anger, etc., that thought form is automatically recorded in our conscious memory and it sinks down into the subconscious where it ferments - particularly so, if the wrong is not righted at the time. Thought forms of this kind may ferment in the subconscious for years and eventually generate the so-called "complexes" and other mental and psychological disorders. If we have enough of these complexes buried in our make-up, we gradually lose our poise and become nervous, sometimes neurotic.

We live in the digital and information dominated times. Our social lives are increasingly interconnected. Our private life is shared with people we barely know and with whom we have never been in physical contact. Thanks to the Internet and new communication technologies, our words, actions, or inactions, good and bad deeds demonstrate a propensity to rapidly expand both in scope and impact. A single word or gesture can spread around the globe with a fascinating rapidity and be embraced or fought against by people and groups living thousands of miles away. Our actions can no longer escape the scrutiny and the lenses of an increasingly expanding social environment.

The old sense of privacy and security is facing increasing challenges not only from our immediate surrounding, but from all over the world. Though we may try to hide behind the computer screen, all our online activities are constantly recorded and can be made discoverable at any time. If discovered and our possible hypocrisy and dirt put into public light, we would find ourselves overwhelmed by a heavy baggage of shame, fear, and anger. Through Confession, however, we have a priceless opportunity to release the emotional energy in the buried complexes so that it evaporates and is no longer in a position to cause us trouble. The necessity to release such adverse emotions is paramount to our personal serenity, our physical, emotional, and mental health, as well as to success in our enterprises.

Sometimes, we indulge ourselves in malicious thoughts and entertain ourselves in the belief, as pointed out in chapter two, that pernicious thoughts not followed by actions are harmless, shame free, and can be continued because nobody can see them, and therefore judge us. But, as said before, this kind of thinking is far from being right. Though it is true to say that our mind is a hermetically secured space where we can feel safe, because only there we can still indulge in thoughts of any kind without being discovered, this mind safety cannot procure us an absolute refuge for quietude if what we keep in it are only reprehensible thought forms that would cast shame on us if discovered. As our lives are more and more interconnected, as our creative thought power is increasing, we are speeding the time when we will become able to create with our words and transmit our creations via the power of emotion, as previously pointed out. The fact that our words and acts are now capable of spreading over the globe and affecting as many people as made possible by the Internet should give us a glimpse of what the creative power of thought and word could do. Indeed, we are approaching a time when our thoughts will become as real, clear, and tangible as any of the objects of the outside world we now perceive through the physical senses.

At present, when a thing or a color is thought of, the image of that thing or color presented by the memory to our inner consciousness is but a dim and shadowy one compared to the thing or color itself. The time is coming closer when there will be a marked change in this respect. Our thoughts will be subject to the call of the Inner Power and not mere reproductions of outer objects. When, for instance, we will say "red," or speak the name of an object, a clear and exact reproduction of the particular shade of red of which we are talking, or of the object to which we refer, will be presented to our inner vision, but it will also be quite visible to the audience. There will be no misconception as to what we mean by our spoken words. Thoughts and ideas will be as alive as visible so that hypocrisy and flattery will be completely eliminated. This, however, does not mean that we will be perfect. Far from that; good and bad will still coexist in each of us and often rubbing each other uncomfortably, but we will be seen exactly as we are. There will be no place to hide, neither behind a computer screen, nor in the sanctuary of our mind. The question is: will we be prepared to be seen as we truly are?

Confession is both a panacea and a shield for us in the present era and in the upcoming next. For the present, Confession helps us purge remorseful thought forms and feelings from our consciousness, while supporting our effort to transform our lives by changing the way we think. As a shield, once we have learned to accept ourselves as we really are and are intrepid enough to assume responsibility for our good deeds and wrongdoings, Confession can shield us against any attempt from the outside world to use our shortcomings to shame us, to bully us, or to blackmail us.

As discussed below, once we have confessed our transgressions and made a resolution not to recidivate, we should leave the past behind and carry on with the course of our lives. In the future, on the other hand, the image-powered-word era will be both reassuring and threatening. In the first case, we will be reassured that we are still humans, capable of doing good and bad, and therefore learn how to accept ourselves as we really are, while striving to better ourselves. In the second case, if we are not capable of assuming the control of what we generate and store in our mind, our thoughts will be easily discovered and exposed to the world. The possibilities for us to be subject of public shaming, blame, and stereotyping would be proportional to the level of control, or lack of, we exercise on our thought, for our thoughts that are generated to impact others will produce such impact regardless to whether we so intended or not. Moreover, we will not be able to hide or misrepresent our bad intentions, which could bring more fear, stress, and guilt to us. By practicing Confession now, we set ourselves on the path of a life without guilt for the past, anxiety for the present, and fear for the future.

A question may be asked: what if we don't trust the priest, or minister with confession? The answer to this question resides in the understanding of the *ratio legis* and the scope of confession. The underlying premises in this question assume that a priest, a pastor, or a member of a clergy has the power to forgive wrongdoings (sins). These premises are based on two biblical directives, the aspects of which can also be found in other religions. But, as will be seen below, these premises have led to wrong assumptions. The first directive comes from the book of James and reads: "*confess your sins to each other and pray for each other so that you may be healed. The prayer of a righteous person is powerful and effective*" ([13]). The second comes from the gospel by John and reads: "*receive the Holy Spirit. If you forgive anyone's sins, their sins are forgiven; if you do not forgive them, they are not forgiven*" ([14]).

Let's take a closer look at these two scriptures. First, the directives from the book of James imply that if someone does something that causes him/her to feel ashamed, remorseful, and fearful (sin) and is sorry for

---

[13] James 5:16
[14] John 20:23

his/her sins; if s/he makes a resolution not to commit this or that wrong again, and then confess to someone in whom s/he has faith and receive their sympathy and assurance that this wrong will not be held against the penitent, this fact would make the penitent feel easier in his/her conscience (healing). The person to whom such confession is made is naturally expected to be a person for whom the penitent has a profound respect and love (righteous person), and s/he will stand toward the penitent at that moment as the representative of God, and to the end that the penitent shall feel very much relieved for having received sympathy from such a confessor. This mark of sympathy and the fact of having a witness will strengthen the pact the penitent has made with his/herself not to commit the sin in question again. If confession is made and received is such manners, it makes sense that absolution so obtained can undoubtedly have a very beneficial effect.

What this scripture does not say, however, is that the confessor (righteous person) has the power to forgive (to erase) sins. Indeed, priests, members of a clergy, or a trusted person don't have by their own the power to cleanse someone else's conscience from complexes caused by transgressions. No mortal individual has such power for the same reason that a person, even the most loving one, cannot digest the food eaten by someone else. The same as the task of digesting food falls on the person who eats the food, so is it with the power of cleansing one's conscience; that is, only the person who has committed wrongdoings can rid him/herself of the sting of thought forms and feelings resulting from wrongdoings. What cleanses the penitent's conscious and eradicates the pictures of wrongdoing from his/her heart and mind and leaves them clean and stainless is the feeling of remorse, of deep and sincere sorrow for what s/he has done, and his/her resolute to change. The logic of this assertion can also be found in the ancient Talmudic Tabernacle. In fact, from the ancient Hebrews' practices and traditions, when someone had committed transgressions and wished to cleanse his/her conscience, s/he had to bring living offerings to the temple and sacrifice them on the altar. The sacrifices were rubbed with salt before being placed upon the Altar of Burnt Offerings ([15]).

We all know how it smarts and burns when we accidentally rub salt into a fresh wound. This rubbing of

---

[15] Exodus 27

salt onto the flesh of offering sacrifices in that ancient Mystery Temple symbolizes the intensity of the feeling of burning and of remorse, of deep and sincere sorrow for what we have done, which at the end eradicates the thought-forms of shame and guilt from our memory and leaves it clean and stainless. Similarly, as under the ancient Talmudic dispensation, transgressors were justified when they brought to the Altar of Burnt Offerings a sacrifice which was there burnt, so in modern times, as discussed below, by scientifically performing the act of scientific confession, we can wipe away the record of our sins. Finally, let's notice that in the Ancient Hebrew Tabernacle transgressors were justified not by the word of the high priest, but by bringing living offerings and burning them on the Altar as a sacrifice for their transgressions. By extension, the penitent in today's world should also sacrifice his/her personality and pride on the altar in the presence of his/her Inner God, feel the fire of remorse and regret burning these offers in his/her soul, therefore purifying him/herself from shame, confusion, and frustrations resulting from wrongdoings.

The above point is not meant to minimize the role of trusted people we may turn to when we are overwhelmed by possible repercussions of our wrongdoings. What it means is that the clergy or the trusted person, if they can freely and in good faith stand as witness for the penitent's confession and resolution not to repeat a transgression, only have the power to give assurance to a transgressor that his/her wrongs will not be used against him/her. Such an assurance is a big relief everyone would welcome in order to continue his/her life on a constructive path. Moreover, since wrongdoings that charge our conscience are often based on our free will, they are the effects proceeding from causes of which only a transgressor can trace the origins. This is another reason why only a transgressor, not a priest, a pastor, or even a trusted person, can rid him/herself of the causes the consequences of which s/he suffers. All can be expected from confessors is to show sympathy for and give assurance to a repenting penitent.

Secondly, with respect to the assumptions from Saint John's gospel, the question this verse raises is whether in this instance Christ was giving his disciples the discretionary power to forgive or not forgive sins, or was he reminding them one of his most important teaching: *"forgive one another just as God forgave us"*. But if we link this verse to another Saint John's verse that reads: *"If you do not believe that (in) I AM, you will indeed die in your sins* ([16])*"*, it becomes clear that Christ was indeed reminding his friends the value of forgiveness, but also underlying the truth that the power to rid our hearts and minds of shame, remorse, and complexes comes from the Inner God, the I AM, of which Christ said existed before Abraham (the father of all nations, races, and people) and which he told his disciples the Holy Spirit will help them remember. While calling upon his friends to forgive each other, Christ made it clear that only *I AM* (Inner God) can cleanse one's sins. The mission the disciples were untrusted to assume was not to forgive sins, the task only God can perform, but to teach humankind how to find and believe in I AM, the Inner God, so that their transgressions may be forgiven. As quoted seven times in Saint John's gospel, I AM is the bread of life; the light of the world; the door; the Good Shepherd; the resurrection and the life; the way, and the truth, and the life; the true vine. This is the real and fundamental teaching of Christ.

Unfortunately, like many uplifting practices,

---

[16] John 8-24

Confession has been abused of by ecclesiastical agents and by trusted individuals in many ways. In some cases, penitents were betrayed by those whom they confessed to, which resulted in facts of confession being disclosed to the public and penitents being shamed, humiliated, or even severely punished publicly. In other cases, religious clergies arrogated themselves the authority to refuse confession to repentant transgressors, whom they deemed unforgivable for the nature of their sins. In many other instances, innocent people were forced to confess inexistent wrongdoings just to end, not being forgiven, but on the brazier. By betraying penitents, the clergy discredited itself and corrupted something of such purity and value. By denying confession to overwhelmed souls, they usurped the power reserved only to God. In either case, NO PENITENT SHOULD BE DENIED THE OPPORTUNITY TO REPENT and ALL REPENTING SINNERS DESERVE MERCY.

Richard Wagner illustrates the intricacies of Confession in his opera Tannhäuser. In this dramatic masterpiece, Heinrich Tannhäuser, one of the troubadours, a mastersinger and a member of sacred order, was in love with the innocent and pure Elisabeth. Heinrich had suddenly disappeared from the circle, leaving his lover in anguish and despair. Having spent a year in the magical underground realm of Venus, the goddess of love, which was considered one of gravest and unforgivable sins, he longed to return to the human world. During a singing contest dedicated to love, Tannhäuser, while aiming to win back the heart of his once abandoned girlfriend Elisabeth, his thoughts were still on Venus. During his replies to the other singers' words, Heinrich betrayed his most kept secret by breaking out into his prize song to Venus, to the horror of the guests. The troubadours drew swords and charged against Tannhäuser, but Elisabeth threw herself between the parties to protect Tannhäuser and begged the knights for mercy. The Landgrave pronounced his judgment: Tannhäuser would be forgiven if he joined the pilgrims on their way to Rome to do penance. Tannhäuser was ragged and weary as he took the way to Rome to show his devout penitence. Once in Rome, he witnessed and rejoiced to see so many people pardoned for their sins. But when his time came to receive forgiveness, his hope turned into despair when the Pope proclaimed that he could no more be forgiven for his sins than the papal staff bear green leaves again. Left without hope, all he wanted then was to return to Venus. Meanwhile, Elisabeth has died while praying for Tannhäuser to be forgiven by God. When he learned about Elisabeth's death, he implores her to continue praying for him in heaven and collapsed dead. As dawn broke, another group of pilgrims arrived from Rome, telling of a miracle: The Pope's staff has blossomed. Heinrich Tannhäuser's sins were forgiven by God himself who sees in the penitent's heart and mind. For the Pope, being human and sinful like all humans, he cannot forgive sins, because he has no such power.

The most delightful news in this regard is that Confession does not have to be made to a priest or a minister, anyway. It can be made directly to the person who has been wronged or to any trustworthy person. But the most secure and the most effective way to confess our wrongdoings is to our individual Inner God. It is worth noting that, in the same above cited example of the Jewish Tabernacle, when someone had committed a grievous crime and fled to the sanctuary, s/he found safety in the shadow of the Altar of sacrifice, for there only the divinely enkindled fire could execute judgment. S/he escaped the shame and scorn from the society by putting him/herself under the hands of God. Similarly, when we can't rely on someone else for Confession and when we are scorned and shamed by the society because of our shortcomings, we can reasonably and safely find refuge in the Sanctuary of our Inner God, in the presence of whom we cannot fear to be judged, rejected, or persecuted when we acknowledge our wrongdoing and confess our transgressions. There, we can be sure to obtain forgiveness, for when we confess to God and renounce wrongdoings, "*though our sins are as scarlet, they shall be white as snow.*"

This confession to the Inner God is what the schools of the Western Wisdom call "Retrospection", which means to look at ourselves. When we perform Retrospection, we look at ourselves in the mirror of our conscience to see our true reflection in it. But, unlike the religious confession, Retrospection is both scientific and spiritual. It helps us turn the gaze not only on our wrongdoings and helps us rid ourselves of them, but also provides us with an opportunity to appreciate our good deeds and incentivizes us to persist in the good direction. Therefore, it important that we learn how to perform this exercise.

After retiring for the night, we begin with relaxing our body in the same way as described in the section on

Concentration. This is very important, because when any part of the body is tense, the blood does not circulate unimpeded; part of it is temporarily imprisoned under pressure. As we all know the benefits of good blood circulation, the maximum effort to connect to our Inner God cannot be made when any part of the body is in tension. Once the body is relaxed, we begin Retrospection by reviewing the scenes of the day IN REVERSE ORDER: first, the scenes of the evening, then the events of the afternoon, and lastly, the occurrences of the morning. The reason for this is that when we look at ourselves in the mirror everything is reversed. If the pictures of our workday were reflected in the mirror, the last images of the evening would stand in the first position, followed by those of afternoon, and so forth. If we were to work with or delete these pictures, we would undoubtedly begin with those in the front line.

As previously mentioned, everything we do, see, hear, touch, say, think, or feel during our wake time is recorded either on our voluntary or conscious memory, or on our subconscious or involuntary memory. During Retrospection, we endeavor to picture to ourselves each scene of the day as faithfully as possible, to reproduce before the eyes of our mind all that took place in each voluntarily pictured scene, with the objective of judging our actions, of ascertaining if our word conveyed the meaning we intended or gave false impression, or if we overstated or understated in relating experiences to others. We review our moral attitude in relation to each scene. We judge ourselves, take blame where blame is due, praise where merited, and learn the causes behind our actions.

It is a foregone conclusion that we cannot continue evening after evening to perform this living sacrifice without becoming better in consequence and ceasing, little by little, to do the things for which we are forced to blame ourselves when we have retired for the night. By doing so, we consciously learn to overcome our weaknesses, we also make a very real advance in morality, justice, and equal treatment of others. Even if we fail to correct our actions, we derive an immense benefit from judging ourselves, thereby generating aspirations toward good, which in time will surely bear fruit in right action.

One of the benefits of Retrospection is to eradicate the injurious habits by giving us the power to control the thoughts and emotions that cause them, and eventually make their gratification impossible. During Retrospection, we try to suffer exactly as we have made others suffer through our dishonesty, cruelty, intolerance, or what not. Because of this suffering we learn to act kindly, honestly, and with forbearance toward others in future. Thus, in consequence of the existence of this beneficent state, we learn virtue and right action. When we wake up the next day, we will be free from bad habits, for at least every evil act committed is one of free will. The tendencies to repeat the evil of past days remain, though. This is a good thing, because we must learn to do right consciously and of our own will. From time to time these tendencies will tempt us, thereby affording us an opportunity of ranging ourselves on the side of mercy and virtue as against vice and cruelty. But to indicate right action and to help us resist the snares and wiles of temptation, we have the memory of remorse and of burning feelings resulting from the expurgation of evil habits and the expiation of the wrong thoughts, desires, and acts from the Retrospection of the night before. If we heed that feeling and abstain from the particular evil involved, the temptation will go away. We will have freed ourselves from it for all time. If, on the other hand, we yield, we should prepare ourselves to experience keener suffering than before until at last we have learned to live by the Golden Rule, because the way of the transgressor is hard. Thus, in addition to cleansing us from our faults, this exercise helps us become better and better every day, but also contributes to the building of a good memory.

As we become aware of this valuable exercise, it is an excellent idea to extend the principle of Confession or Retrospection to the preceding years of life so as to clear up the complexes that have become embedded in the makeup and which frustrate success. This process might be called "Delayed Retrospection" and can be done best in writing. That is, we sit down and systematically write out a general outline of the events of the past which have involved fear, anger, shame, etc. We may go as much as possible in the past and continue until the whole life has been retrospected. Gradually, a wonderful mental and emotional release will be found. And this will be reflected in improved conditions affecting work and material needs. This writing should be done secretly and later destroyed to avoid the temptation of opening old wounds.

Taken as a whole, Retrospection when practiced at the end of the day as discussed, comes with many benefits: (1) thorough relaxation of the body; (2) increase in power of devotion and feeling for truth; (3) knowledge of how the

Law of Cause and Effect operates in life; (4) restoration of harmony in the body more quickly than would otherwise be done; (5) increase in our power to remember; (6) progress in attitude and development; (7) thought control, which must result from a disciplined effort to retrace the events of the day.

A question may arise as to whether retrospection is necessary when we repent immediately for undesirable words or actions. However, it seems obvious that it would be impossible to reap all the above benefits by simply repenting during the day for undesirable deeds, even if we had the time to do so. The fact that we repent immediately for having hurt another person is all in our favor, of course, but how could any sincere person help do that? Where there is no sincere repentance, there would likely be neither memory of the experience nor incentive to real repentance in the evening. In the same respect, let's also realize that constant attention to the events of the day can be detrimental rather than helpful. We cannot be productive at work if we are constantly in fear of losing our job, nor can we have a fulfilled life if we are constantly afraid of making mistakes, or under fear of going to hell. In fact, when we are too anxious, constantly ruminating over faults and feverishly anxious to eradicate them, when we are ever intent upon ourselves to see if we are growing, then we are in point of fact exactly as a little kid who has planted a seed and daily scratches the soil from the tiny rootlets to see if the seed is growing into a plant. We know that by such ill-advised anxiety the kid frustrates the very object s/he wishes to attain; and when we are constantly putting ourselves in the limelight and hyper critically reviewing our shortcomings, we are also defeating the end we seek to serve and deferring the consummation of our hopes. Retrospection exercise gives us all necessary scope for criticism. To keep chiding ourselves throughout the day has the same effect as if someone else were picking at us all the time.

One other important point to make is that when we perform the exercise of Retrospection, we should give ourselves over to the feelings of regret and remorse with our whole soul; we should endeavor to shed tears of fire that may burn into our very innermost being; we should make the cleansing process as thorough as possible, to the end that we may grow in grace thereby to the utmost. But, having finished the exercise, we should consider the incidents of the day closed and forget all about them: -

forgive and forget -, save in so far as they demand restitution of something, the making of an apology, or such subsequent acts to satisfy the demands of conscience. And having thus paid the debt, our attitude ought to be one of unfailing optimism, for we can confidently declare *"si deus pro nobis quis contra nos"*- or "If God be for us, who can be against us?" By such attitude, we die daily to the old life and we are born each day to walk in the newness of our daily life, for our desire and thoughts are thus renewed and ready to serve a higher aim in life than the day before. On the other hand, if we indulge in regrets and remorse during every waking hour as we sometimes do, we are outdoing the purge and miss the chances to learn new lessons and grow. Thus, remorse and regret when continually indulged in have the same effect as the continuation of antibiotic use after the infection has been eliminated. Such attitude is also a denial of the power of the Inner God to forgive our transgressions. For these reasons, it is as dangerous to our mental, emotional, and physical health to indulge indiscriminately in feelings of regret and remorse as it is potentially fatal to physical well-being to continue taking antibiotics when infections have already been cured. Critical thinking should govern in both cases.

Following the same line, and while we are discussing regret and remorse as applied to the problem of soul-growth, with their effect on our mental, emotional, and physical health, we may also profitably mention the effect of regret directed into other channels. Sometimes, we live with regret as with a boon companion, we take it to bed with us at night and get up with it in the morning; we take it to the office, shop, or church; we sit with it at meals, we nurse it as the most precious thing in our possession, and we would sooner part with life itself than give up our regret for this, that, or the other thing. As a vampire sucks the vital fuel of its victim and feeds upon it, so perpetual thoughts of regret and remorse concerning certain things become a demon acting as a vampire and drawing the very life from the poor soul who has shaped it, and by the attraction of like for like, it fosters continuance of this morbid habit of regret. Such emotions are subversive of both physical and mental health, and consequently detrimental to all effort for success in life. Instead, let us cultivate an attitude of optimism in all things and faith in the Inner Power. The only way to build a world we dream of is to work for it. This work begins with our relentless effort to better ourselves on physical, mental, and emotional levels. But such things are as fundamental to us as they are fragile, which makes conquering them a Daily Quest.

Conclusion

Our life force comes from the Power Within, the Inner God. True success in life requires a reasonable degree of physical, emotional, and mental health; that is, a balanced personality. For us to conquer a Sound body, a Sane mind, and a Soft heart, it is essential that our personality, our mind, and our will cooperate with the Inner Power and refuse to make restraining thought forms. If anything interferes with the flow of this life down through the personality and the body, ill health results.

It is possible to imprison the Inner Power behind a cloud of wrong thought-forms - false beliefs - so that the constructive flow of the vital energy from within is decidedly reduced. When we make destructive thought-forms (those of fear, anger, selfishness, etc.) which limit us, when we allow ourselves to believe that evil has power over us, and when we believe that we are limited in life and always will be, all these things tend to imprison the flow of the vital force from the Inner Power into our conscious mind and personality.

The Daily Quest is all about the dismantling of the destructive and depressing mental cloud and the forging of an instrument with which this cloud of wrong thought-forms can be pierced and replaced. This instrument consists of new thought forms of confidence and strength, of optimism, success and sureness, and of faith in the omniscience and omnipotence of the Inner Power that all good things are attainable. The exercises of Concentration, Meditation, and Prayer are our powerful gears in this Quest. They not only shield us through challenges and serve as communication channel between our conscious mind and the Command Center (Inner Power), but they also help us build new thought-forms along this line. These, in return, will combine themselves into a composite thought-form of great strength and potency, resulting in good health, new opportunities, and success in life. The Daily Quest is, thus, the path of self-discipline: winning control over our thoughts, words, feelings, and deeds. Against this, our personality constantly rebels and offers all kinds of excuses to prevent its accomplishment, but we are never forced to heed them. We realize that the exercises of Concentration, Meditation, Prayer and Retrospection require the use of Will, the highest aspect of the Inner

Power, to control thoughts and emotions for a definite, sequential period of time. Hence, for this reason, along with all the others mentioned in this essay, successfully performing them can be a big victory for the Inner Power; a victory that would give us strength and power.

This journey, however, is an individual business. No religion, guru, teacher, or master can establish a connection between our personality and our Inner Power, nor can they perform the above described exercises for us and transfer us the benefits that come with the performance. The Quest is open to everyone who can dare, regardless to whether we are religious or not. If we believe that we only live in this material realm and death ends all things, this Quest is a great deal in that it calls us to work as hard as possible to make the world a better place, here and now, by becoming better ourselves every day. If we believe that upon death our fate is either heaven or hell, this Quest gives us the power to choose our *post mortem* destiny, while helping us work every day for the progress of all beings. If we are believers of the law of rebirth, also called reincarnation, by undertaking this Quest, we set ourselves out for a better future life and karma and speed our time for the Nirvana. To engage in this Quest is to understand that we are here

like young birds pushed off the nest if we don't do it
ourselves.

We now know about the tools we have for the
Quest. We also know about all the support and help we can
request and receive from the inner and the outside worlds.
But, like the riddle of life and death, the Daily Quest is an
individual undertaking. Each of us must find answers to the
many questions that keep her/him awake and apply them
to her/his individual specific situation. We may try and fail
many times; we may sometimes hurt ourselves trying, but
every attempt is a step forward, for by trying we learn how
to fly by our own; and for that, our wings need first to
undergo training.

References

1- I Corinthians 2:11

2- John 1:1-5

3-https://www.encyclopedia.com/humanities/encyclopedias-almanacs-transcripts-and-maps/arche
4- https://www.ligo.org/science/GW-Stochastic.php

5- https://phys.org/news/2017-07-giant-atoms-gravitational-big.html#jCp
6- Psalm 139:7-12

7- https://www.nobelprize.org/prizes/medicine/1904/pavlov/lecture/

8- https://www.ncbi.nlm.nih.gov/pmc/articles/PMC1665254/

9- https://biologydictionary.net/muscular-system/

10- https://biologydictionary.net/cardiac-muscle/

11- John 8:48-59

12- Romans 12:2

13- James 5:16

14- John 20:23

15- Exodus 27

16- John 8:24

Made in the USA
San Bernardino, CA
27 December 2018